SEX

AND

OTHER TOUCHY SUBJECTS

BY SHELLEY LESSIN STOCKWELL

This book has been named "Gift of the Year Award" winner by the International Family Health Council of the Pacific.

"Reading Shelley's poems makes one wonder if he is reading the Rubiyats, Don Blanding, or the musings of a Guru. It's GOOD!"
—Dick Wheeler
The Hue and Cry

"Simple, clear, and to the point . . . one liners a scream."
—Dr. Tom Rische
The South Bay
New Times

"Shelley Lessin Stockwell has done it again! She reminds us that through our foibles and tough times, we are magnificent, perfect, and funny just the way we are."
—Dennis Briskin
Ghost Writer

"Shelley has an eerie talent for writing MY very thoughts... To enjoy this book is to truly enjoy myself."
—Kris Blake
Magic Mirrors

"In a word, 'Fantastic.'"
—Maria Cort

"I never got into poetry very much, but when I read a few of Shelley Lessin Stockwell's poems, I just had to read all of them. They are absolutely riveting.
—Paula Suarez

For e.e. Cummings

e.e. Cummings changed my life.
His words, blooming fresh from white pages,
spoke to my germinating words.

e.e. Cummings, when I learned that you died,
(Two years later than the fact)
I cried. And some of me died, too.

Then, time later than an uphill mile,
my words were birthed anew.
And with scrawls of mind scraps
upon my pads,
I bravely laid my tender heart
and dreams
and foibles out
to air
hoping you would care.

"Lest we forget the human dilemma shared by all the living, not quite in silence anymore."

- Nancy Cummings De Forêt,
Daughter of e.e. Cummings

e.e. Cummings . . . on being a poet.

A poet is somebody who feels, and expresses his feelings through words.

This may sound easy. It isn't.

A lot of people think or believe or know they feel - but that's thinking or believing or knowing; not feeling. And poetry is feeling - not knowing or believing or thinking.

Almost anybody can learn to think or believe or know, but not a single human being can be taught to feel. Why? Because whenever you think or you believe or you know, you're a lot of other people: but the moment you feel, you're nobody-but-yourself.

To be nobody-but-yourself — in a world which is doing its best, night and day, to make you everybody else — means to fight the hardest battle which any human being can fight; and never stop fighting.

As for expressing nobody-but-yourself in words, that means working just a little harder than anybody who isn't a poet can possibly imagine. Why? Because nothing is quite as easy as using words like somebody else. We all of us do exactly this nearly all of the time — and whenever we do it, we're not poets.

If, at the end of your first ten or fifteen years of fighting and working and feeling, you find you've written one line of one poem, you'll be very lucky indeed.

And so my advice to all young people who wish to become poets is: do something easy, like learning how to blow up the world — unless you're not only willing, but glad, to feel and work and fight till you die.

Does this sound dismal? It isn't.
It's the most wonderful life on earth.
Or so I feel.

— A Poet's Advice, 1955.

Sex and other Touchy Subjects

Cover and Inside Photos by
Jon Nicholas

Illustrated by
Jeff Bucchino

Additional Art & Photos by
Ewa Carlsson,
John Bruecker,
Bryce Stockwell,
Karen Ottoson
& Dennis Briskin

CREATIVITY UNLIMITED PRESS
30819 Casilina
Rancho Palos Verdes, CA 90274 U.S.A.

©1990

by Shelley Lessin Stockwell

All rights reserved. No portion of this book may be reproduced in any form or by mechanical means without the written permission of the publisher, except by a reviewer who may wish to quote brief passages in connection with a review for a newspaper or magazine.

ISBN: 0 912559-12-8
Library of Congress Catalogue Card Number: 88-071940

Printed in the United States of America

To my mother Irma Kapilese Lessin
and my father Irving M. Lessin.

Rest in Peace.

Mommy and Daddy
   you pooled your genes
   (random as ping pong balls)
   and out I came.

Mommy and Daddy
   actors in the movie
   with my name.

Mommy and Daddy
   I reflect your strengths
   and self-deceits and
   cut the umbilical
   to love myself

   complete.

Acknowledgements

To my beloved, Jon Nicholas, I give my heart and gratitude for your generous loving and encouragement.

My love and deepest thanks go to Bruce Rische, Dr. Alex Lessin, Dr. Tom Rische, Sophie Lessin, Dennis Briskin, Jeff Bucchino, Ewa Carlsson, Judy Wolkovitch, Carol Kerster, Dr. Joan Kelly Lessin, Bryce Stockwell, Judy Pastel Walker, Dr. David Walker, Gabriela Moeller, Gilda Whited, Vicky Sample, Rene Ramirez, Rosemarie Ramirez, Betty Greenburg, Alicia and John Maniatakis, John Bruecker, John Sample, Dr. John Goode, Lydia Goode, Consuelo and Rick Chavez, Janet Levering, Pat Salmon, Bob Landis, Bob Morales, Dr. Robert Lewis, Kristin Blake, Chris "Mad-Dog" Moeller, Betsy Moreland, Steve Robinson, Sarah Mandel, Helen Lessin, Richard Vogl, Candice Unruh, Sandra Hatakenaka, Winnie and Ed Self, Jessica Morris and Don Bay. Each of you contributed to making this book a reality.

And finally, I extend my heartfelt appreciation to my family, personal friends, and all my faithful reader friends for your continuing support and affections.

Thank You For Being My Friend

You are a surprise party!
Gushing, overflowing in abundant beauty.
You,
who gives so freely,
not taking bows or credit;

You,
whose very nature is an
endless hidden treasure.

You, whose silent loving
echoes thunder through the valley;
you have set my cells a-dancing.
Whirling,
smiling,
spinning;
a riot of elation,
giddy in my joy.

I am dizzied and bedazzled,
touched deeply by your caring;
your kindness is the music
and my heart sings to your song.

Yes, you are a surprise party.
For you open secret doors in me
and I recall afresh
that all that matters

is love.

I LOVE YOU,
Shelley

This Poet

This poet knows your loneliness.
This poet knows your need.
This poet's reaching out for you
with love
and not with greed.

You may receive all I can give,
now could be our time;
or old scars cut within you, Dear,
could keep your heart from mine.

God bless you now
my precious friend;
I wish you peace and caring.
My deepest wisdom feels with you
and the defenses you are wearing.

Getting It On

Of all life's interests and pursuits,
a quest for power, a quest for loot,
intellectual aggrandizement,
wearing labels for advertisement.
Doing drugs, doing religion,
procrastinating or making decisions.
Your line of work or philosophy,
loving your dog or your bonsai tree:

What you really want, what you're hungry for,
is touch, love, sex: toujour l'amour.
Nature commands life to make itself anew,
you are of nature and you know it is true.

So don't delay in deluded diversions,
getting lost in projected excursions,
love and sex is all there is.
Ask your heart.
Ask your kid.

I Am You

Look at me.
I am your eyes:
Seeing life go moving by.

Listen to me.
I speak for you:
the silent thoughts you know as truth.

Breathe with me.
Let's share our air:
in a truly human love affair.

Yes,
I am you from
core to crust.
If you can't trust me:

Whom can you trust?

Stop, Look And Learn

We are only mirrors for each other.

In your fear and hesitancy,
you reflect my fear and hesitancy.
In your love,
I see my loving.

We are each the teacher
and the student.
We can see in one another
our leasts,
our beasts,
our bests.

Look well into my eyes and reflect.

Photo by Jon Nicholas

Two poems to go please,
one over easy,
and one
well done.

Photo by Jon Nicholas

TABLE OF CONTENTS

LIFE

LIFE	1
BORN DAY	2
SUNRISE	3
IT JUST DAWNED ON US	4
ANCIENT SOUP	5
OLD SAYING	6
FRUSTRATION	7
QT(pi)'s	9
MT. ST. HELEN'S: ROCK AND ROLL	10
ME	11
SPHERE	12
GOOD POEM	13
WAR GAME: IT'S THE RAGE!	14
TWISTED	15
THAT'S CLEAR, I'M OBSCURE	16
I THINK, THEREFORE I AM, I THINK	17
ILLUSIONS	18
GUY LOMBARDO TO PUNKEST ROCK	19
WE ALL HAVE OUR AXIOM TO GRIND	20
I'LL CALL YOU IF I SEE YOU AGAIN	21
HOW TO CREATE A VOID	22
LIE	23
HORNSWAGGLED	24
SO WHAT	25
INTEGRITY	26
YOUR MOMMY DONE TAUGHT YOU	27
YOU NEVER LISTEN	28
LOOK AT ME	29
REMEMBER	30
WHO AM I?	31
CONSUMING PASSION	32
DEJA VU	33
THIN ICE / LOSS OF POWDER	34
THERAPY	36
PEELING	37
A SCHIZOPHRENIC IS NEVER ALONE	38
BE HERE NOW	39
LET'S PLAY	40
THE BEST CAUSE	41
CREATIVITY	42
YES! I'M POSITIVE	43
NEGATIVE TRANSFER	44
YOUR BEAUTY IS IMMENSE	45
WONDER FULL	46
SEASONS OF THE DAY	47
LIFE IS A ROSE	50

Poems marked with this logo are included on Shelley's cassette Sex and Other Touchy Subjects

LOVE KNOTS

WE EXIST	53
HOW TO LOVE WITHOUT GETTING EMOTIONALLY INVOLVED	54
HEART SICK	55
BROKEN DREAMS	56
GOING, GOING, GONE	57
STORM	58
CACOPHONY	59
VIDE-OUCH	60
MY HUSBAND IS A TREE	61
DIVORCE	62
WARM SLIPPERS	63
SLEEPING GIANT	64
I PAIN, HURTING YOU	65
DIS ALLUSION	66
STALL-OUT	67
COUNTDOWN TO CRACKUP?	68
WHAT YOU SAID	69
BEGINNING OF GOODBYE	70
FARE THEE WELL	71
WHY ME?	72
MAD	73
TANTRUM	74
WHO DO YOU THINK YOU ARE?	75
IF YOU WANT TO BE LITTLE	76
GRUDGE	77
BEWARE!	78
I WAS GOING	79
IT'S NOT WORKING	80
DOOR MAT	81
YO-YO	82
ALONE	83
THIS YEAR IN REVIEW	84
I TOLD MY TRUTH	85
RUPTURE	86
I AMTRAK-ING YOU	87
LOVING YOU	88
C.B.	89
PRESERVING THE PIECE	90
HORSE PUCKY	91
FISHERMEN	92
MOOSE	93
BLEEDING TREE	94
MY MISTER	95
WORDS	96

SEX

SPLURGE	99
ANIMAL/CRACKER	100
SEX WITH YOU?	101
MATE	102
GIFT	104
ANIMAL MAN / GENTLE MAN	105
AN-ATOM-ME	106
AFTER GLOW	107
AFTER SEX	108
MALE ENERGY	109
COME IN	110
VIDE-OH	111
ECSTASY	112
ORGY	113
WHEN?	114
FONDLE OF YOU	115
TWO BIRDS AFAR	116
ABSTINENCE	117
I MET YOUR WIFE TODAY	118
IMPOTENCE	119
PURR PET YOU ATE	120
MORE ASS	121
SEX IS F...D	122
IN THE PUBIC DOMAIN	123
I AM NOT A WIND UP TOY	124
FUZZY AREA	125
UDDER CONFUSION	126
DATING GAME REJECT	127
IS THERE LIFE AFTER LUST?	129
RUSSIAN CAVIAR	130
MY PRINCE	131
VIRGIN TERRITORY / CHASTITY	132

LOVE

L.O.V.E.	135
I LOVE ME	136
WEDDING VOW	137
YOU OF MY DREAMS	138
WANT: ADD	139
IT MATTERS	140
SHOPPING TRIP	141
YOUR PARTY	142
SPONTANEOUS COMBUSTION	143
IF I WERE CLEAR	144
GALE	145
DON'T INNER FEAR	146
LOVE TALK?	147
YOU	148
HEART SONG	149
MELT	150
YOU ARE A PART OF ME	151
I WANT TO DRIFT IN YOUR EYES	152
I AWAKEN STILL	153
TONIGHT	154
DO YOU REMEMBER?	155
I WANT	156
DEVIANT	157
STRIPPED NAKED	158
LAND OF PROMISES	159
COMMUNICATION	160
MOTORCYCLE MAMA	162
TRAIL BLAZED HER	163
JOURNEY	164
EAST COAST	165
CAN'T WAIT	166
SHEJONNY	167
BLOOMIN'	168
CHARMING / DISARMING	169
EN-TRANCED	170
I WANT TO DO YOU IN	171
POEM	172
FOR YOU	173
CRYSTAL	174
CONCERT OF JON	175
HEARTLAND	176
MERGED AND MELDED	177
PLAYMATE	178
IN HARMONY	179
YOU ARE A JOY!	180
JUST THE SAME	181
HOLY-DAY	182
I HAVE BEEN LOVED BY YOU	183
MY CAT	184
BANKING ON US	185
HA	186

MOM, DAD, & APPLE PIE

NOSTALGIA	189
MY PRIZED POSSESSION	190
CLASS OF '62	191
DIRTY LAUNDRY	193
I LEARNED EARLY	195
THE BEST SHE COULD	196
DADDY DIED	197
GHOST	198
HEAVY	199
THANKSGIVING	200
FAST FOOD	201
BLETCH	202
MY MOM WAS FAT	203
THINK ABOUT LIPSTICK	204
LOOKING GOOD	205
SHOPPING MALL CRUISER	206
HOARDING YOUR MONEY	207
LOOSE CHANGE	208
YOU ARE A TURTLE	209
RECREATIONAL VEHICLE	210
R.V. RESORT SALES PRESENTATION	211
DAM	212
115 IN THE SHADE	213
ZION/YONKERS/VEGAS	214
SEDONA, ARIZONA	215
BIG SUR	216
STEWARDESS SONG	217
YULE SURVIVE	219
RUBBER BABIES	220
SOME FLUFFY GIRL	221
SETTING SON: RISING SON	222
LITTLE MAN	223
BRYCE	224
MISS CONCEPTION	225
TEARS / A MINICURE	226
NEIGHBOR	227
LAST NIGHT	228

FRIENDS & FOES

FRIENDS	231
31 FLAVORS	232
GIVE IT A WHIRL	233
YOUR BEAT	234
CHILD	236
WHO?	237
IF YOU WEREN'T SHY	238
RESCUE	239
PEACE TALKS	240
IF THE SHREW FITS, SWEAR IT	241
UNCLE CHARLEY	242
LOOK WHO CAME TO TOWN	243
DON'T NEGLECT	244
DON'T EAT WITH YOUR MOUTH FULL	245
THE MORE YOU OBSERVE	246
DO WHAT EVER	247
TOM	248
THREADS	249
C SECTION	250
LINNEA BRITT	251
MY GRANDPA	252
FIJIANS	253
MAN	254
THOSE EYES!	255
BATTLE WITH TIME	256
DE PART	257
BLURRING TIME	258
OHH, THOSE HANDS!	259
ENGLISH SHOWERS	260

RELIGION & DRUGS

GOD	263
CLOSE TO THEE	264
ENLIGHTENMENT	265
THE RELIGION	266
WHO DOESN'T LOVE A FLOWER	267
REALITY	268
LOVE DRUNK	269
OBSESSION	270
NO CON TEST	271
RECURRENT TRAINING	272
HELL LOOSE SIN O GIN	273
OH BROTHER	274
SPRINKLED SPAGHETTI	275
HALF TWO	276
SHOCK THERAPY	277
YOUR BODY	278

DEATH

TIME	281
TUTANKHAMEN	282
FUNERAL HOME	283
IT'S GREAT TO BE ALIVE	284
ACCIDENT	287
THE ROOSTER	288
HEART ATTACK	291
THE HELPING HAND	292
FRIGHTENED	296
CAN'T WORRY	298
PRISM GIRL	299
ABOUT THE AUTHOR	300

LIFE

PAIR O DOCS

My life is so exciting
I hope I can live through it.

Born Day

Birthday; your day.
Celebrate you.

Consider the miracle
that you are here,
though understanding is unclear.

Your mom and dad one day got cozy
and put you in a place real rosy.
You started out as a one-celled critter
who didn't require a baby sitter.

But,
   expansive you,
spread and divided,
Making your mother quite lopsided.
And,
   shortly after,
out you came;
a fuzzy person
without a name!

Isn't it wild you showed up that day
and not your little brother?
And what were you doing just before
you fattened up your mother?

Your fixtures could have been the opposite gender.
And any color, your skin so tender.
You might have arrived in a Bangladesh hovel
thinking of food as something novel.

So celebrate life,
   you're a Freudian slip,
You could have been lost 'twixt the cup and the lip.

Birthday; your day.
Celebrate you.

Sunrise

Startled shadows spew in linear
escapade.
Ms. sunshine stretches;
flicking on her angled floodlight
with a yawn,
laughing the shadows to crags and
crevices.
"They're not too bright." she says,
shedding new light.

It Just Dawned On Us

Lick luscious morning
wonder wet with glisten.
The silence speaks
if we just listen.

The sun cracks clouds in bold array
teasing darkness into day.

Our bedding pod blooms us afresh
and we emerge like babies' breath.
Thank you, God, for this day glorious.
Our hearts connect with Earth:

Euphorious.

Ancient Soup

Etruscans and Phoenicians,
Sinestras and Sinaquas,
Levites, Mongols and many Moors.
Pot shards, polyglyphs,
bones and crumbled walls, recall.
Buried scratch marks
on the flesh of times past,
recalling people just like us
who lived, loved, shat and spake,
and might have eaten birthday cake.

The earth is our scrap book
upon whose pages we gaze
at forgotten momentos of a living soul or civilization,
illuminated for a flicker and dropped
as a pressed flower upon the pages.

I look at the sun beam
flooding this ancient room,
and see countless swirling flecks
frantic in the light.

Each speck is one past human life.
Always they fill everywhere - air,
yet, have been hidden from my sight.

Oh, let me, in another day recall,
that as I breathe,
their memories enter and leave,
giving me the life force that is mine.

I stand at my sunny window
looking at crumbling walls
and take a deep breath;
an inspiration.

Photo by Jon Nicholas

There's an old saying

I'm thinking up.

Frustration

FRUSTRATION is the "F" word,
FRUSTRATION is a scream.
FRUSTRATION is the hair
in the middle of your mint dream.

Late for the meeting you took four years to plan,
(The garage door wouldn't open, your toilet overran).
Lost your wallet with your credit card collection,
cop pulls you over for a smog inspection.
Lets you go, you punch it in reverse,
now his Harley Davidson needs a hearse.

FRUSTRATION, no satisfaction,
spinning tires without any traction.
Voice recorder puts you on hold.
Don't talk back. Do what you're told.

An illegal alien, in mashed up Ford, totals your new Mercedes,
hands you her baby, smells like gin,
then keels over and dies
with a grin.
The baby won't stop crying.
Your teenager's always lying.
Your mate is dead or dying.
Your boss says you're not trying
(and you are).

Trying, trying, trying.
It's FRUSTRATION, there's no denying.
Computer virus, disk drive crash,
you're over billed and under cashed.
Polly won't grip,
can't find your keys,
pantyhose slipping down past your knees.

(Continued)

You come home sick, the house is a mess,
your husband's wearing your favorite dress.
Your office calls, says you've been fired
so your ex-husband could be hired.
Getting cozy, at last in bed,
your husband moans, "I love you, Fred."

FRUSTRATION is the promise that doesn't deliver:
a digit away from the lottery winner,
a telephone that eats your dimes,
waiting for an hour in the wrong line.

The station's out of gas,
the bank is out of cash,
you and your best friend clash.
He says you're a pain in his . . .

FRUSTRATION:
Anger with no place to go.
The kitchen's on fire,
your plants won't grow.

NO! NO! NO! NO!

FRUSTRATION is the "F" word,
FRUSTRATION is a scream.
FRUSTRATION is the hair
in the middle of your mint dream.

Q T π's

"I was thinking today I was losing it."
"Did you ever have it?"

"Are you from around these parts?"
"I live smack dab in the middle of these parts."

"These pants someone gave me are too tight."
"You should have them lose weight."

"Stop it! Put me down!"
"Ok . . . Your mother wears combat boots!"

"Me want kiss."
"You kiss monster?"
"Yes!"
"Then me no want to kiss you."

Mount St. Helens: Rock and Roll

Hey, red-headed mountain
with the flat top,
when the lava-naughty earth-heart
let it fly
did you cry?
or
Did you roll over
in laughter?

Me

What makes me run?
Marriage, cleaning,
(a demanding son.)

What makes me sad?
Others in pain,
the loss of my dad.

What makes me stay?
Praise, kindness,
getting laid.

What makes me tense?
Criticism, anger,
self defense.

What makes me, me?
What I hear, feel,
taste, touch, see.

What makes me know?
A peaceful rain,
sun, wind, air, snow.

Sphere

Earth is worth
her girth in mirth.
The merry land
where we lie and stand.

She sucks us all in gravity,
regardless of color
or depravity.
Glues us on water,
snow and ground,
regularly makes us
come around.

She runs hot and cold,
is third from the sun,
and weighs in at 6.6 sextillion short tons!

For her global support
and latitude,
(forgive me for the platitude)

I offer Earth my gratitude.

Good Poem
(for Goody Two Shoes)

Good morning
Good day
Good night.

Good boy
Good natured
Good and bright.

Good friend.
Good self starter.
Good worker.

Good husband.
Good lover
Good father

Good citizen
Good soldier
Good fighter

Good god
Good heavens
Good grief
Good bye

War Game: It's The Rage!

Fat cat, smiling bureaucrat,
   strategic planning diplomat,
   run chess games played by smooth faced pawns
   on deserts, oceans, manicured lawns,
   jungles, islands, airways, bars,
   local turf or distant shores.

The young pawns die to do it right,
   for home or glory or the thrill of the fight:
   to take a castle, or a king;
   be knighted for the suffering.

Behind his desk the gamesman grins,
   carefully sips a glass of gin,
   counts his money and
   plans his win.

No elder statesman can berate
this conscientious diplomate.

Check Mate

Slowly, mankind has learned the score:
   fodder can't father anymore;
   widows and cripples sift the rubble
   and wonder if life is worth the trouble.

The grim truth hurts humanity.
Change begins with you and me.
We know the game.
We know the score.

Let's not fight war anymore.

Twisted

That thought that's clear
while in my brain,
gets lost for words
awong the lay.
It falls out tisted
on my twongue.
Oh how I dear
that I sound fumb.

That's Clear. I'm Obscure

Pick up the mattress;
drink from the spring.
Call him collect;
He'll buy you that ring.

Tickle her fancy;
make her titter.
Should you stand for
a baby sitter?

If it's hot,
why call it chili?
Can you slap somebody silly?

Settle down and
live it up,
what do you do
with a loving cup?

Are there legs
on a walking stick?
Can a jello mold
make you sick?

How does rush hour
cause congestion?
Put off procrastination;
fight aggression.

Even in schools,
fish never sleep.
You could be in left field
if you count sheep.

If there are inns
in an outing,
outs in an inning,
where is the end
of a poor beginning?

I Think, Therefore I Am, I Think

Thoughts arc,
words converge,
trainwreck sentences
fall of the end of clarity
and crash to bits.

An army of little grays
run frantic,
picking up pieces,
looking for blueprints and superglue.

I smile sweetly and keep talking.

How little is known of our brain.
To think about thinking is to
wrap a mist about a mist.
How do you know?
How do you grasp moonbeam thoughts to
look upon them in your hand?

Your voice is a printout of a
control room in good working order.

I probe your skull package
hoping to enter through your eyes
or, perhaps, run backwards upon
your clear sentences to touch their source.

My thought fragments scatter like dust
as I look for one well lighted room without
transient armies knocking the shit out of my
progression of words and concepts.

"Thank God I'm not senile," I say, knocking on wood.

"Who's there?" I answer.

Illusions

Waves, contractions,
love affairs:
ebb and flow,
come and go.

Nothing different,
nothing the same,
moments change moments,
no matter our game.

I took a photo
of a little boy
holding a blanket,
laughing in joy.
Now he's a man
with that same
funny face.
Not one moment
of his truth
I can trace.

And who was the one who took his pictures?
She was gone before we missed her.
I've been in her company since the front of her life.
I meet her at my mirror,
yet, not for a second does she look the same
(and I never can outstare her).

So seize the moment, if you will.
Understand, if you've got the notion.
My perceptions blurred by mystery,
and life's uncertainly commotion.

Guy Lombardo To Punkest Rock

Guy Lombardo to punkest rock
is just a diversion; just a crock.
For we all march in the same brigade.

Some boast about the progress made;
some look back with dewy eye;
some clump along with mournful sigh.
Some do a jig along the way.
Some beg to leave.
Some beg to stay.

Yes, our styles may vary
or the cut of our hair.
   Our colors subtle
   or with blinding flare.
Yet, there is no difference;
it's how we pretend.
We're all on this march from beginning to end.

And our teeth and hair will come and go.
Our locks get frosty; white as snow.
We'll grow and ripen and come to bloom.
It matters not the marching tune.

Guy Lombardo to punkest rock.
Is just a diversion; just a crock.

We All Have Our Axiom To Grind

Rules are roadblocks created by the powerful to keep the timid from success.

Photo by Jon Nicholas

I'll Call You
(If I See You Again)

Women, chest pieces
you slide around,
chickie-bored moves
on a cheater-board ground.

You're starving for love,
so this game takes its toll;
as you lie to each piece
and you plan your control.

Oh, you're the winner in gamesmanship,
top dog and power;
as your heart dies a death
of an unnurtured flower.

How To Create A Void

Avoid

Lie

Your life is a glorious lie
bordered in the social graces
framed by the latest "stuff."
Shallow banter is your muzak.

You, a good boy scout, loyal and true,
chained in silent hysteria
to family, success and chewing food with a vengeance.

Sex, snatches of stolen candy,
hastily gobbled, breaking rules and hearts.
Love, a silent drum, pounding your head
against the walls of your pretend life.

Outside your door is a sky as big as the ocean,
and a man (with your name) trying to tell
you that
the only truth of your life
is you.

Hornswaggled

To tell the truth
(and that's no lie)
I wouldn't feed some alibi.

No, I ain't joshin';
(and that's no bull)
I wouldn't think to pull the wool.

Of course I'll give it to you straight.
(really I won't hesitate)
Avoid the issue? Fake, deceive?
Why, honestly! Whom can you believe?

So What

"Pragmatically, truth is what is,"
he said matter of factly,
"It's no quiz."

The artist says, "Truth is illusion I observe."
The poet says simply, "Truth is words."

"Truth is concept."

"Truth is guess."

"Truth, I believe, is just faith at best."

"Truth is what I create it to be
by employing power and strategy."

"Truth becomes us when we feel 'right'."

I say; Truth is a diamond reflecting light;
moves invisible (answers no name)
and is more evolved
than our human brain.

Integrity

Tellers of truth
don't clear their throats
or second guess
or stab with jokes (just kidding).

Tellers of truth
listen with their hearts,
talk with their eyes,
are often loved; seldom despised.

Truth sayers are awake;
aren't constipated,
don't have belly aches.
Attend self-conducted seminars.
Listen well to their inner voices:
Nude warriors,
amidst manipulative finery,
pretentions and illusion.

Tellers of truth are each one of us
before we learn
to lie and deny.

Your Mommy Done Taught You

Your mommy done taught you that to compliment is bad.
It'll make you swell-headed, conceited, a cad.
So she'd chide and she'd nudge you - never enough.
She was building character, makin' you tough.

Now you finger my faults with accusing tone.
You don't say my strengths, they get lost in your groan.
You're my critical daddy, a-cluckin' his tongue
over all my shortcomings, the mistakes that I've done.

Your mouth ate a lemon, your eyes squint and glare.
You know more than me about hows, whys and wheres.
You question my info, my timing, my plans,
my cooking, my voice tones, my spending, my fans.

This flower needs sunshine; enough of your shit.
For you I won't blossom 'til you just go and quit
a-dumpin' and gripin' and scrunchin' your face
and admit I'm a winner, I ain't no disgrace.

Stroking breeds kindness, softness and growth.
Warmth and deep caring is what you'll evoke.
If you look with soft eyes and compliment clearly,
I will do my best to please
and I will love you dearly.

You Never Listen

You never listen,
(perhaps your ears are weak)
you never take the time
to acknowledge what I shriek.

You never understand
anything I say,
I can tell by your wrong
answers and the
ignorance you display.

Stop interrupting,
swearing that you do.
Define your terms,
shut up right now.
Listen, I'm talking to you!

You never listen,
(perhaps your ears are weak)
you never take the time
to acknowledge what I shriek.

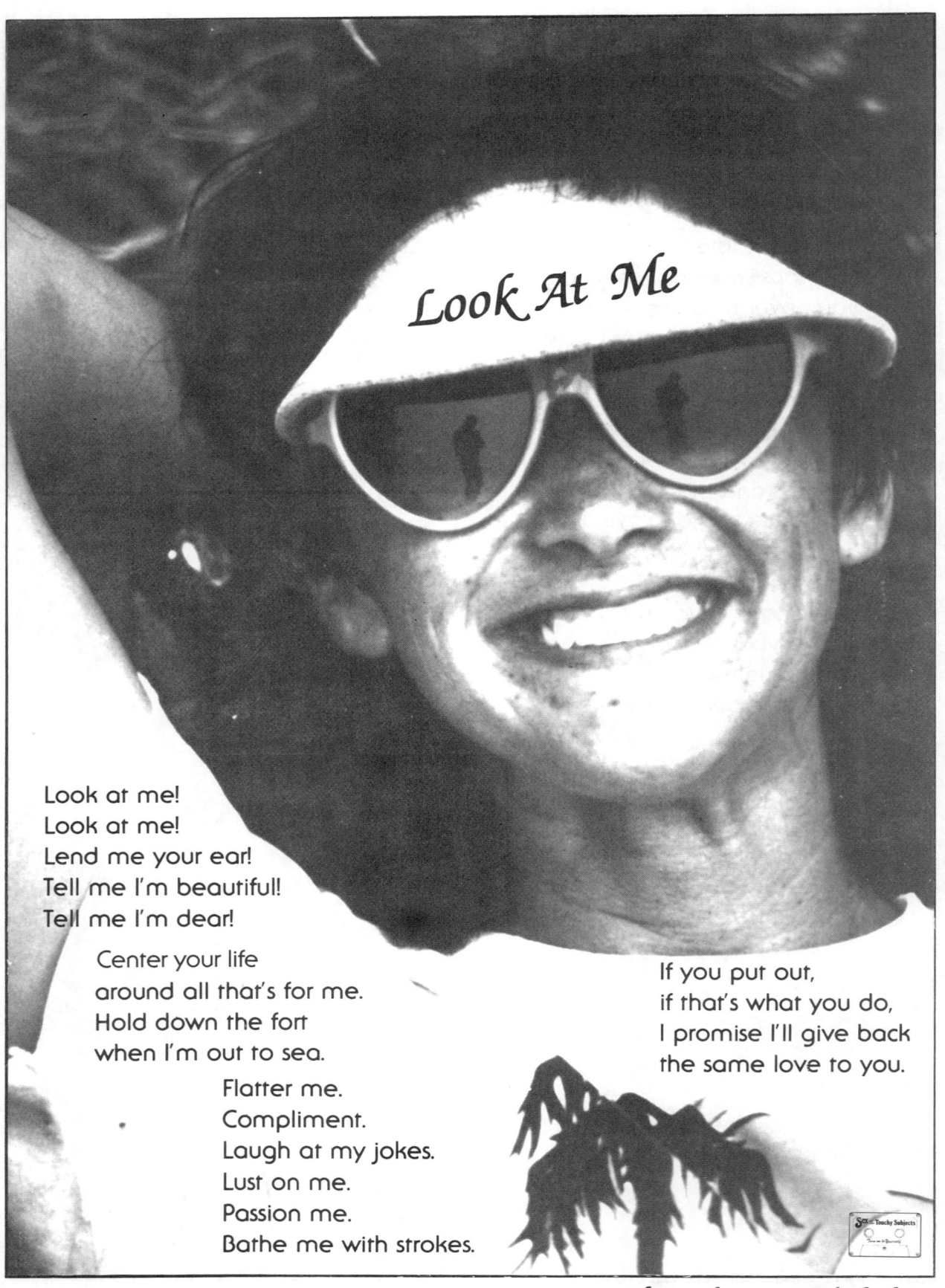

Look At Me

Look at me!
Look at me!
Lend me your ear!
Tell me I'm beautiful!
Tell me I'm dear!

   Center your life
   around all that's for me.
   Hold down the fort
   when I'm out to sea.

      Flatter me.
      Compliment.
      Laugh at my jokes.
      Lust on me.
      Passion me.
      Bathe me with strokes.

If you put out,
if that's what you do,
I promise I'll give back
the same love to you.

Photo by Jon Nicholas

Remember

Remember

that listening to every conversation
is your inner clarity and wisdom.

You may poison your body
(With grass, alcohol, sugar, pills, or tobacco.)
You may poison your mind
(with obsessions, manipulations or put-downs.)

But no matter what your age,
or your situation,
you know the truth of your life
and the people around you.

And,
more importantly,
you know exactly what you need to do
to make your life
the happiest, healthiest life you can live:
mentally,
physically,
spiritually
and emotionally.

Remember

Who Am I?

Who am I when I don't pretend
to sway or sell or impress?
Who lives under my latest "do"
and the style that I choose to dress?
What voice is my own; not my parents' or friends'?
What's the most guarded fear I try to defend?

The more that I hide me, the harder I work,
the less I feel joy: And it's really no quirk.
Pretending is fun, except for the part
of living the mask, instead of my heart.

So I accept my real voice, I have no greater friend
who knows me this well and is there 'til the end.

Consuming Passion

Massive buying by the masses.
Gotta give us credit.
Gimme, buy me, take me, send me.
Please Mom, can I get it?

To buy, buy, buy,
makes me so high;
If I can't have it
I'll just die.

Boutique, department store, catalogue,
swap meets, home sales, on the job,
television marketing, unsolicited call,
bury me near the shopping mall.

Wave some plastic near my head.
If I don't move, you'll know I'm dead.

Deja Vu

Biggle jiggle joggle bink,
changing lifetimes in a blink.
Anger, pain, hurt and such,
push and pull, repel and touch.
It ain't free 'til you give it away.
You ain't free 'til you come to stay.
Rules and pride and acting strong;
the humility to say I'm wrong.
Ache and tear to find your way.
Deciphering the shades of gray.
Will we ever meet again?
Did we ever? Where and when?
Obsess, repeat and chant your name.
Is this real or just a game?
Going down, why don't I stop?
With all this bullshit suffering slop.

Loss Of Powder: Snow Skidding

Snow
dancing in swirls and curtsies
across the pavement.
Flakes
spinning patterns
at the windshield.

Frost-skirted trees,
slide past me
and nod;

as I
(in a mental whiteout)
spin wheels
on frozen wastelands of my defenses:

Leaving me cold.
Leaving me skiddish.

When you are walking on thin ice,
you could easily be in hot water.

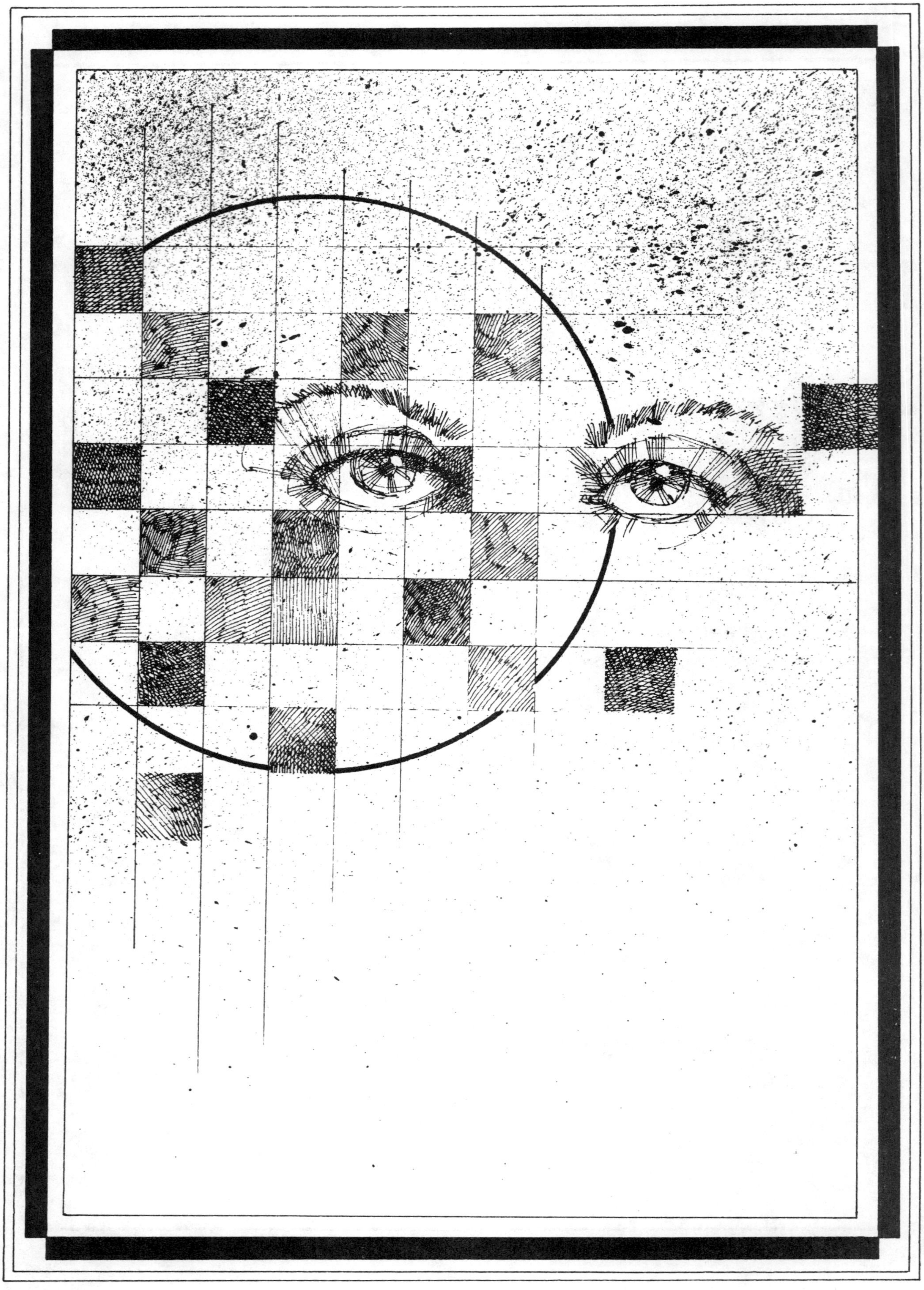

Therapy

Punching, pounding, fighting it out.
Rip and tear, scream and shout.
Pieces, bits, go flying by,
in this battle ground called I.

My head said no, my heart said yes,
inside I was a royal mess.
The battle plan of this ancient war
acted out many times before,
had left me smiling in a mold
hoping that I wouldn't explode.
And then I came across your door;
you bade me to "at least explore"
the place in me where I was snagged.
You didn't condemn, or scold or nag;
but listened long and listened well
to the morbid details I did tell.

Air started seeping from my hot air balloon
as I sat and wept inside your room.
And bit by bit we slowed it down;
the bloody war, the smiling clown.
And quietly put the soldiers to rest
with a calm acceptance in my breast.

The warring fractions they're each me:
We live together physically.
I'm a tapestry made of thread
woven perfectly in my head.
Tough and soft;
girl and woman,
body, mind:
now interwoven.

Opening yourself is a peeling.

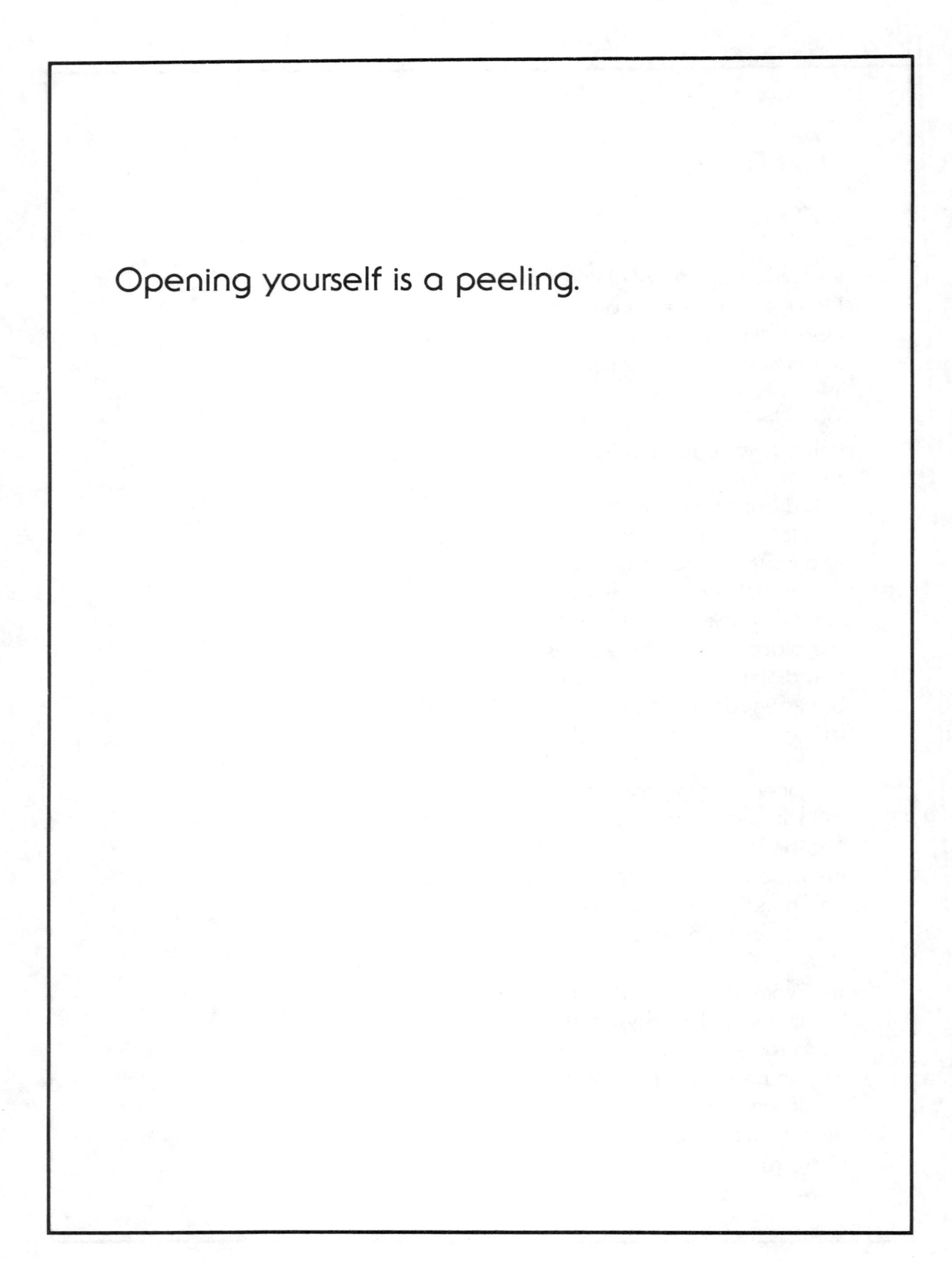

A Schizophrenic Is Never Alone

Some would call me schizo,
others say I'm spaced.
I see myself as flexible,
varying my pace.

Some would say I'm ballsy,
others that I'm crass.
I say I'm assertive,
I stand up to the task.

The facts of life,
the way it is,
the truth throughout the land.
It's only the way one looks at me
that determines where I stand.

Be Here Now

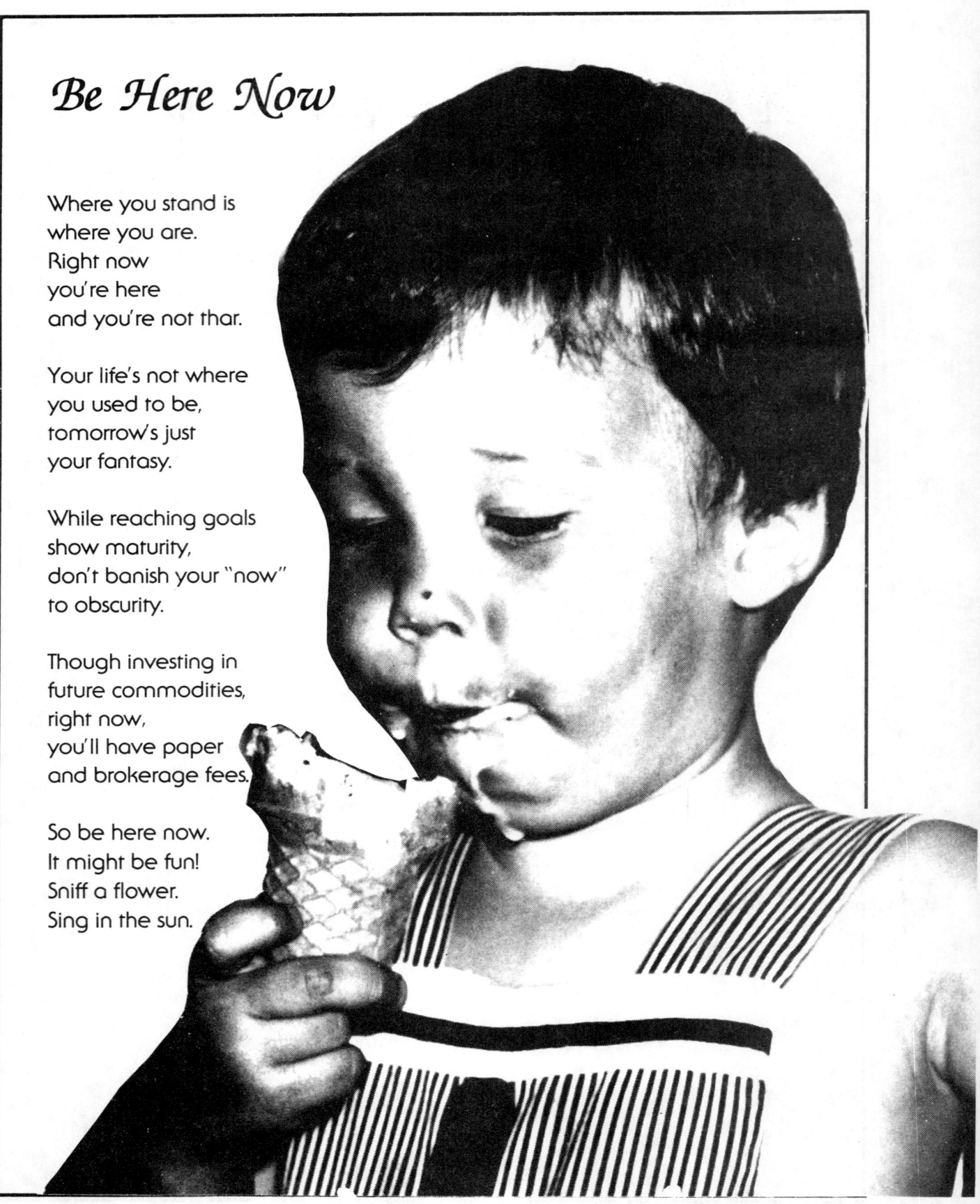

Where you stand is
where you are.
Right now
you're here
and you're not thar.

Your life's not where
you used to be,
tomorrow's just
your fantasy.

While reaching goals
show maturity,
don't banish your "now"
to obscurity.

Though investing in
future commodities,
right now,
you'll have paper
and brokerage fees.

So be here now.
It might be fun!
Sniff a flower.
Sing in the sun.

Photo by Jon Nicholas

Let's Play

Come on,
let's play!
Get carried away,
flirt all day.
Right now is a gift
wrapped in our ribbon.
We'll be free
with nothing hidden.
Come on,
let's play!

The Best Cause

Be cause

Creativity

Dehydrated thoughts,
saltine crackers in the desert,
ideas gone dry,
scattered, spinning in lost wind,
settling like dust.

And each is a seed that any
instant, blooms tender in the
wastelands.

What a wonderful idea!
(It grows on you)

Yes! I'm Positive.

Sunshine wonderful
Absolutely yes!
I am feelin' fine; complete
I am at my best.

I hear that you were crying:
slashin' mental wrists.
Give your head a twist about.
Put your grief to rest.

Once I was mistaken,
sad, on overload.
Now I'm positively bent;
and I'm not even stoned.

Say sunshine wonderful,
absolutely yes!
When you're happy, feelin' fine,
you can't be depressed.

Life is a conspiracy
guaranteed ecstasy,
abundant love to satisfy
all the needs of you and I.

Want it, watch it happen.
Enjoy absurdities,
giggle, chortle, laugh aloud,
start slappin' at your knees.

Sunshine wonderful.
Absolutely yes!
I am groovy, feelin' fine.
I am at my best.

Negative Transfer

Where a discouraging word may
be heard.
Where one gives up, quits
because of fear.
Where negatives prevail
and it's set up to fail.
Where? Over there,
 it's prohibited here.

Your beauty is immense when you give up your pretense.

What kind of full are you?

Wonderfull!

Photo by Jon Nicholas

Seasons Of The Day

Spring (morning)

Dizzy bedazzled,
dreamy love drizzle,
drippily dingy,
your lips make me sizzle.
Dally delectable,
delight my gee whizzle.
How do you do it?
That is the quizzle.

    Today is a life time
    richly in season,
    flowing and rolling,
    teasin' and pleasin'.
    Your mind is a garden.
    You reap what you sow.
    Happily moving,
    that's how we grow.

Summer (afternoon)

Higglety jingle,
mix and mingle,
puppy dogs,
lady man.
Gender bender,
use your gender,
Love you baby,
yes I can.

Joy, joy
the high priced spread,
tickles monkeys,
in your head;
who twirl and roll
in formal attire
lauging like
a house on fire.

    Today is a life time
    richly in season,
    flowing and rolling,
    teasin' and pleasin'.
    Your mind is a garden.
    You reap what you sow.
    Happily moving,
    that's how you grow.

(Continued)

Fall (twilight)

Speckled sun
in bold array;
dancing shadows,
end of day.
Melt your eyes to
love crumbs deep,
I'll dance in
with tickle feet.

Your beauty is divine,
immense,
ripened colors,
no pretense.
Into wishin'
quiet kissin',
sunlight fading,
gentle shading.

>Today is a lifetime
richly in season,
flowing and rolling,
teasin' and pleasin'.
Your mind is a garden.
You reap what you sow.
Happily moving,
that's how we grow.

Winter (night)

Easy, slow,
watch us grow.
Time moves us gently
in his palm,
as our faces
wrinkle some,
and you and I
our dreams become.

So come on over.
Lap on me.
I give to you
my loving cup.

Photo by Jon Nicholas

Life Is A Rose

Life is like a rose,
fragrant in its blooming,
thorns for humility,
color for vitality,
kissed by sun and earth.
Washed by rain.
Giddy with breezes,
growing in seasons,
dropping as gentle petals
as new roses come and go.

Life is a rose
resplendant and radiant for its hour.
We are each a rose:
a perfect flower.

LOVE KNOTS

RAIN DEAR

We Exist

We exist,
   we're here to stay,
until,
   of course,
you go away.
Our time together is real,
   you see,
no matter who you're pretending to be.

We set the course of our time in this space.
We dance to the tunes that we play.
If we repeat non-corrective,
   with our hearing selective:
We choreograph it that way.

Instead of your mate;
You pretend I'm your mother.
I forget who you are
and I think you're my brother.

We are used to fill
hollows of an earlier age;
to patch up old hurts,
to vent out old rage.

Childhood is a dream.
As adults we awaken.
Your life's not your dream;
do not be mistaken.

Yes,
we exist,
   we're here to stay.
Unless,
   of course,
you go away.
Our time together is real,
   you see,
no matter who you're pretending to be.

If we each trust our senses,
we can come from our truth

and each moment will be a surprise;
of energy, movement, excitement and sighs
and the mystery coming from our newborn eyes.

How To Love Without Getting Emotionally Involved

Immerse in work.
Call each other jerk.
Scrub the floor.
Fix the door.
Talk about your kids.
observe the "didn'ts"; ignore the "dids."
Don't look in the eyes.
Slip in little lies.
Turn off your ears.
Hide your fears.
Be busy.
Be quizzy.
Read your book.
Start to cook.
Drug and TV away.
Make the other pay.
Talk on the phone.
Give your dog a bone.
Think of another.
Pretend they're your mother.
Keep rules rigid.
Keep bed frigid.
Number of years can
be your tome;
then you can be
together alone.

Photo by Karen Ottoson

Heart Sick

My heart was damaged
at least once that I know
because I seem to remember it so.
By a tiny rejection
or the hope of some dream
or the death of my Dad
or not being prom queen.

Beaten into submission,
the calluses spread
'til my soft little heart
sat there practically dead.
And my life's become safe
with the comforts of home,
my toys,
my husband,
and my child;
I'm alone.

Yet there's nary a thing
that I know I can do
to save my sick heart,
do you?
Once I pried it open to give to a man,
but he got scared and away he ran.

So my heart pounds,
rhythm to my brain,
hurt and callouses:
we're one and the same.

Broken Dreams

Down to the bottom of the heap,
my foolish heart took a quantum leap.
Under the rubble of broken dreams
my heart started rupturing at the seams.

Going Going Gone

It's all the things you didn't say
that finally pushed me far away.
I'm starving for touch.
Starving for tell.
I'm not getting nourished.
I'm not feeling well.

Your intentions are kind,
you like me, I'm sure.
Yet, your silence diseased me
and, perhaps, there's no cure.

I kept trying to tell you
the best that I could,
but, I couldn't change you.
It did me no good.

Your desire lies dormant.
Your passion is gone.
Yet, you adore me with stroking
and a sweet gentle song.

So I'm going away,
don't feel your vital stuff.
I'm not leaving to hurt you,
I'm just not nourished enough.

Storm

Warm, silent sky
cracks open,
flash and gush and spew.
The raging sky
(topsy turvy),
wracks my sleeping calm.

Stale dreams that bind me;
cracked open by your name.
Is my love willing to risk it all,
or is it just a passing storm?

My quivering heart cracking open,
flash and gush and spew.
Raging passionate desire
wracks my sleeping calm.

How much peaceful solitude
is worth the price of melding our souls?
Warm your smile upon me.
Take away this driving rain, and pain.

I am a seed pod opening.
Your sun and this damn incessant rain
will bring me to new bloom.
But, Jesus, I'm scared.

Cacophony

Cacophony of clatter
blurring me in chatter.
This raging storm within my skull
shows me that you matter.

Vide-Ouch

Partners at the video game
controls. You get the little
man through the maze . . . stomping
out dynomite and keeping him from
being eaten by birds.
I move the pillars up and down, out
of your way, careful not to squish
the little man, trying to squash those
bad birds.

I concentrate so as to
do it right; and raise your
skill level and your score.
"Oops, I goofed . . . squished your
man by pushing the button wrong."
And the pillar smashes him to smithereens.
"That's it! I don't want to play with you anymore,"
you shout, turning off the monitor.
"That's the third time you've smashed my man."

Your words fall through my skull,
a pillar bigger than the Number 1
Wilshire Building. Seems I don't please
you anymore.

"It's only a game," I reply.

My Husband Is A Tree

My husband is a tree
planted silent, guarding me.
The harshest sun, the driving rain,
never will harm me again.

His strength of limb and solid stance
keep him from his finest dance.
Keep him stuck, his feet in clay,
make him mine; he won't go away.

Time and season, and acorn son;
Friends have gone and friends have come.
Flowers blossomed, flowers died;
Clashing waves, rolling tide.

Impassioned once and then no more
in our garden where love was born.
Shaded calm stands over me;
my husband has become a tree.

Lousy coffee is grounds for divorce.

Sometimes a mooring become boring.

The main cause of divorce is marriage.

Warm Slippers

When did our passion slide to warm slippers
scooting silent down the hall?
Was it somewhere between the comfort of
commitment and the predictability of
our mutual kindnesses?
Or between the diapers
or the business accolades?

Together,
we have gathered a colorful bouquet
of friends and stuff.
Old calendar pages leafing us through
anniversaries a-plenty.

I love your thoughtful ways and shelter.
I love you deep and true and
I will love you forever;
even as I go.

And, when our farewells are done
I will remain haunted by the echo
of distant vacant slippers.

Sleeping Giant

Hot lava dormant,
soft rocks sleeping.
My friend,
the thrust of (past)
eruptions echoes
through the hollows
of my memory:

a cock crowing
in a distant village.

I Pain, Hurting You

I pain, hurting you.
Watching your eyes;
side-sniped, sunken.
Your tight mouth
afraid to say
"Don't go away."

I never thought that
we could end
(for there was no rend
we couldn't mend).

Our lust past
now a haunting ghost;
though I vowed
to love you most.

Oh, I pain while hurting you,
as we tear to parts.
I am touched while letting go,
and bleed with you, Sweetheart.

Dis-Alusion

My marriage broke up because
of a stressful divorce.

Stall-Out

My stall-out was the insidious kind;
ruled by calculated logic.
Losing altitude in a numbing silence.
I didn't note the clouds and sun
falling up faster than light speed.

My heart,
imprisoned in walls of small rejections;
my mind,
diverted to intricate tasks
designed to show the world my "O.K."ness.

You are the only witness of my stall-out.
Your heart,
falling through applause,
and women in your bed,
shared my silent desperation.

In your eyes lives the truth of angels
and I am,
once again, reminded
that I can fly.

Countdown to Crackup?

The space shuttle exploded,
seven souls disseminated;
blown to jet-propulsioned smithereens
before our collective eyes.

When we met,
my marriage
was on course;
mechanically correct.
You pushed the trigger,
sparking my padded capsule;
and my shaky marriage
ruptured at the seams,
blowing up before my eyes.

Today,
from the launch pad of our dream,
(the one made of passion and sensitive caring)
when the car didn't start
(and we were late),
you talked to me
(across the bitter snow)
with sarcasm.

Your jagged, implied "stupids" cut me
like glass.
Warily, I witness your explosion.

What You Said Was A Whack On My Head

Thoughts looming bigger than night
crowd my sleep.
Your snores needle the twisted yarn
of my fears.
"I'm not 'in' love with you," you said
"or 'in' lust."
In your eyes,
I've seen quiet night deserts,
with the sun flooding the horizon,
and, I knew, that there is no limit
to our love affair.

Your words, like quicksand,
obscure your eyes and the newly
budding day.

I lie awake,
deafened by the sound of slamming doors
and your gentle snores.

Beginning of Goodbye

You told me of your past loves:
fantastic women whom you held
   and left
   and grieved after
   then moved on.

Their names shift like grains
through my hollow fears and
pile upon the grains of my sweet lovers'
past.

Last night,
when you said that we weren't good
for each other and that I brought
out the worst in you,

your words stung like a sandstorm.

Is this the beginning of goodbye?

Fare Thee Well

If someday
we pass by
one another
on a street corner,
on the freeway,
in the supermarket,
or in a dream,
may neither of us utter
even the slightest
of sounds,
may our hearts not dance
nor an eye
or lid flinch,

for that moment of meeting
will pass just as my
lips have passed away
from your lips.

Why Me?

My touch makes you recoil.
My viewpoint makes you boil.
With all this stress and turmoil,
why hang on to this old goil?

Mad

When I'm pissed off,
I do things faster.
Key stone cops:
cleaning with a vengeance.
Muffling
my complaints
under slitted eyes
   that see nothing.

When I'm mad;
it's always your fault.
."What's wrong with you anyway?"

When I'm angry;
my tizzies are energy spun out
on a dusty race track
burning in the sun.

When I'm ticked;
I don't feel well.
I don't hear the little child
within,
frightened and alone.
Desperate for a friend.

When I'm pissed off,

I forget to love.

Tantrum

The demons are dancing
in and out,
tight rubber bands snapping tension
with their taunting.
"Don't use me.
 Don't abuse me.
 Don't tell me.
 Don't hurt me."
You snit in sniping glares and criticism
the demons laugh with glee
at what you will not see.
You're taking your tension seriously
when it's only naughty energy
breaking free.
Take a deep breath.
Surrender.
Be.

Who Do You Think You Are?

Who do you think you are,
talking to me that way?
Snipy-tongued and caustic.

You don't feel good about yourself.
O.K.

You want to say
muffled "stupids" to yourself.
That's fine.

But I'm trying to walk out of my
"stupid-not-good-enough-what's-wrong-with-you-any-way" shoes
into the love light,
the god spectrum:
the peaceful lands.

Don't talk to me that way.
Who do you think you are?

If You Want To Be Little

Belittle.

Never forgive someone who bears a grudge.

Beware!

You flare,
I scare
and tear.

I go dumb,
sinking silent
in the arms of
numb.
I die
and bleed;
hoping
not to need
your care.

Beware!

I Was Going

I was going to write you a poem
about how much I love you,
about how every time you climax
it's like visiting a town,
brand spanking new,
with everyone smiling for
a parade down Main Street.

I was going to tell you how you,
even with your eccentricities and
temperamental withholdings,
are still my white knight
coming to me in my lost wilderness.

I would have said that I love you
to the breadth and depth of me
(tender me and awkward me
and all the me's in between).

I was even screwing up the courage
to tell you
that I want to be your mate
for always (all ways)
and please, don't leave me.

But, you made me so damn mad
the way you said, "Tell me later,"
I shut down.

I was going to tell you.
I was going.
I am going.

Now, I can't really say.

It's Not Working

It's not working.
You don't talk to me,
and I feel lonely.

You tease me
more than praise me;
and I feel insecure.

Your mouth is tight on the edges,
and I withdraw and
do penance for crimes
I suspect I committed.

No, it's not working.
I'm filling in your silent blanks
with negatives.
I'm closing and running
(in fits and starts)
while you,
absorbed in pot,
and books,
and the earth,
make your own movie
wondering
perhaps,
if it's working.

Door Mat

My heart was your welcome mat
a semi-permeable membrane
for your energy and words

Then, in time,
and familiariity,
you spoke to me
the way you speak
to yourself;
sprinkling putdowns
and sarcasms
and
"What's wrong with you?"

Today,
I didn't hear a word
you said;
the doormat's soiled
by muddy boots.
I'm pulling it in
for spring cleaning.

Yo-Yo

I'm moving out of our dream
and clearing out of your drawers.
I don't think that I can take
this love affair no more.

Red light; green light.
Come here; go away.
That's the little game we play.

When you met me I was married
and also was engaged.
Now I'm only married.
So why are you outraged?

You promised to take me to islands.
I promised a ride cross the sun.
I'm left with a yeast infection
and a hicky the size of my thumb.

Pack 'em up; move 'em out.
That's what our romance is all about.
Each good bye is the final time:
Today is move out number 99.

I'm moving out of our dream
and clearing out of your drawers.
I don't think that I can take
this love affair no more.

When you use that tone,
I feel alone.

Photo by Jon Nicholas

This Year In Review

This year in review,
you say there's nothing more to do.
No use to continue,
it's my move or we're through.

You, my precious mate
have not gone beyond my glance,
and all the times that you stood by, I knew.
And still, sometimes,
your words cut me like a knife
and I withdrew from you.

Darling, can't you see
that you've touched the deepest parts of me.
Your river primal in my nights and days
even as I stumbled in that maze.

You say that you're enraged,
there's nothing more to do
and anger's eating you.

Standing hurt by each abuse,
we both have muttered,
"What's the use?"
Come now.
Let's move to a greater truth
beyond the hurt and fear excuse.

For we've touched each other at the core.
Isn't that what love is for?

I love you.
I want you.
I need you.

I Told My Truth

I told the truth; it made you sad.
I hadn't planned to do it.
I'd hoped you'd see where you are stuck
and pleasantly move through it.

But there's pain in birth
and puberty too.
Growth rips us open
to expand and renew.

Perhaps I should have smiled sweet smiles;
not taken your show to task;
slipping in neatly to your packaged life,
without that kick in the ass.

But my duty to you is as simple as truth,
and if you think I'm not fun anymore
just say,
"That's enough, keep your words in your mouth,"
and quietly show me the door.

I'd rather risk my time spent with you
and lose you to defenses or tears,
than to play deaf & blind to the truth that I feel,
or compromise me with my fears.

I care enough to share with you;
please listen with your heart.
Let's grow closer with reality
and let's not wedge apart.

So, I told you my truth; it made you sad.
I hadn't planned to do it.
I'd rather just love you; this tears me apart;
I hope that our love gets through this.

Rupture

Rupture of my heart's frail walls,
torn apart again;
broken fragments falling down.
It's easy to explain.

My heart is dumb, an animal,
guided with no mind;
stalking for its treasure prey,
mute and deaf and blind.

And I, a tall and noble sort,
with rules and thoughts refined,
was dragged behind my hungry heart;
confused, perplexed, resigned.

I do not know what you have felt.
I cannot read those eyes.
Mine burn too much in stinging tears
to know your truth or lies.

It's not for pride that I despair,
it's not for right or wrong,
it's simply that you've gone away
from my heart that's not so strong.

I Amtrak-ing You

I amtrak-ing you
boarding the train.
(putting the luggage
in the overhead shelving)
I missed the goodbye of your eyes.
Pulling myself
(tightly clutching my heart
to an orderly package of so long).

Clack clack clack
ties and tracks
rolling jiggles me away.

Your face remains tattooed
fresh at the window
framed by your strong, square hands

Clack clack clack
miles and space
my aching yearning
branded by your richly
shiny eyes.

Alone on the train,
I touch the pane.

Loving You

Running wide open
into an airplane propeller
yelling, "Here I come,"
and, "what was that?"
when it was done.

C.B.

Some women like a
slicked-down dude
papered with degrees.
Some like jocks with
sweaty socks and
muscles on their knees.

But give me a gear jammer
with a rig,
who smells of diesel fuel.
A drivin' man with tattooed arms,
and I drip and drool.

Static grit on my C.B.
Gotta get a handle
on why they answer Leadfoot Lil
and ignore me: it's a scandal.

I call for ears in my sweetest tone,
but no one says diddly on their phone.
I beg. I plead. "Just come on back,"
trucker, smokey, lumberjack.

Now Leadfood Lil, she drives the Cads
and mother truckers loony mad.
"Breaker, breaker," her voice rates ten
with all them worldy travelin' men.

Static grit on my C.B.
All alone at 23.
Lil's got em' hanging on the line.
Why, oh why, can't one be mine?

So I'll just sit and twirl my dial,
pedal to the metal and try to smile.
I'm tuned on; won't squelch or hide
'til someone catches my flip side.

Spark my heart, give me a charge.
Spark my heart, park in my garage.
Drive me crazy; drive me sane.
Give me a handle; give me your name!

Preserving the Piece

You told me of your last affair:
How she pursued, her beautiful hair.
Your interest waned, you said, in time.
Yet, she persists, "It's such a crime!"

Another woman in your bed
could never replace me, you said.
Yet, I felt a wedge before you told
of this other interlude so bold.
Time has kept you long away;
for love and tides they move and sway,
taking us through moods and phases,
seeking folks to sing our praises.

So now our love is pulling apart,
but, before you're sure you broke my heart
you should know, that while you were away . . .
I, too, had a new lover come my way.

Horse Pucky

If your cowboy makes eyes at another:
Cut him off at the pass.

He shouldn't have a prairie!

Fishermen

Beware of fishermen
over their limit.
Avoid the temptation,
try to out-swim it.

    You told me of others
    who jumped into your fray;
    I heard your bleak warning,
    but could not stay away.

    You touched me down deep,
    I was lured by your smile,
    hooked by your line
    and your bold manly style.

Beware of fishermen
over their limit.
Avoid the temptation;
try to out-swim it.

    I had learned to be savvy,
    I had learned to survive;
    Yet, I'm compelled to be with you,
    dead or alive.

    So I jumped in head first
    to your gorgeous black net.
    My head was a spinnin'
    and hasn't stopped yet.

Beware of the fisherman
who has your brand of bait.
He could be there for sport,
he could be your soulmate.

    Now I'm caught in your current
    that will not subside.
    Will you make me your pet
    or eat me pan-fried?

Moose

Hanging there, silently glass-eyed, staring at me.
The elegant curving of your fine fur snout.
Your proud antlers spreading like wings.

The thickness of your chest pokes through red brick,
while you, frozen in stark stillness,
watch me eat my trout and mashed potatoes,
on a china plate, with a gauze tied lemon,
to keep the pips from squirting out.

The fish catches in my throat;
damned by your powerful immensity.
Forgive me,
if only I could remember to love you enough.

Your proud antlers spread like wings,
Harris tweed hats dangling on each stretching point.

Bleeding Tree

A tree bleeding from spring,
I have bared for you my limbs
and, as best I could, my soul.

I am making ready
for a long winter
in the silent echoing
of memory.

My mister.
Much missed.
Much mist.

Words can make a tremendous difference in how we say things.

SEX

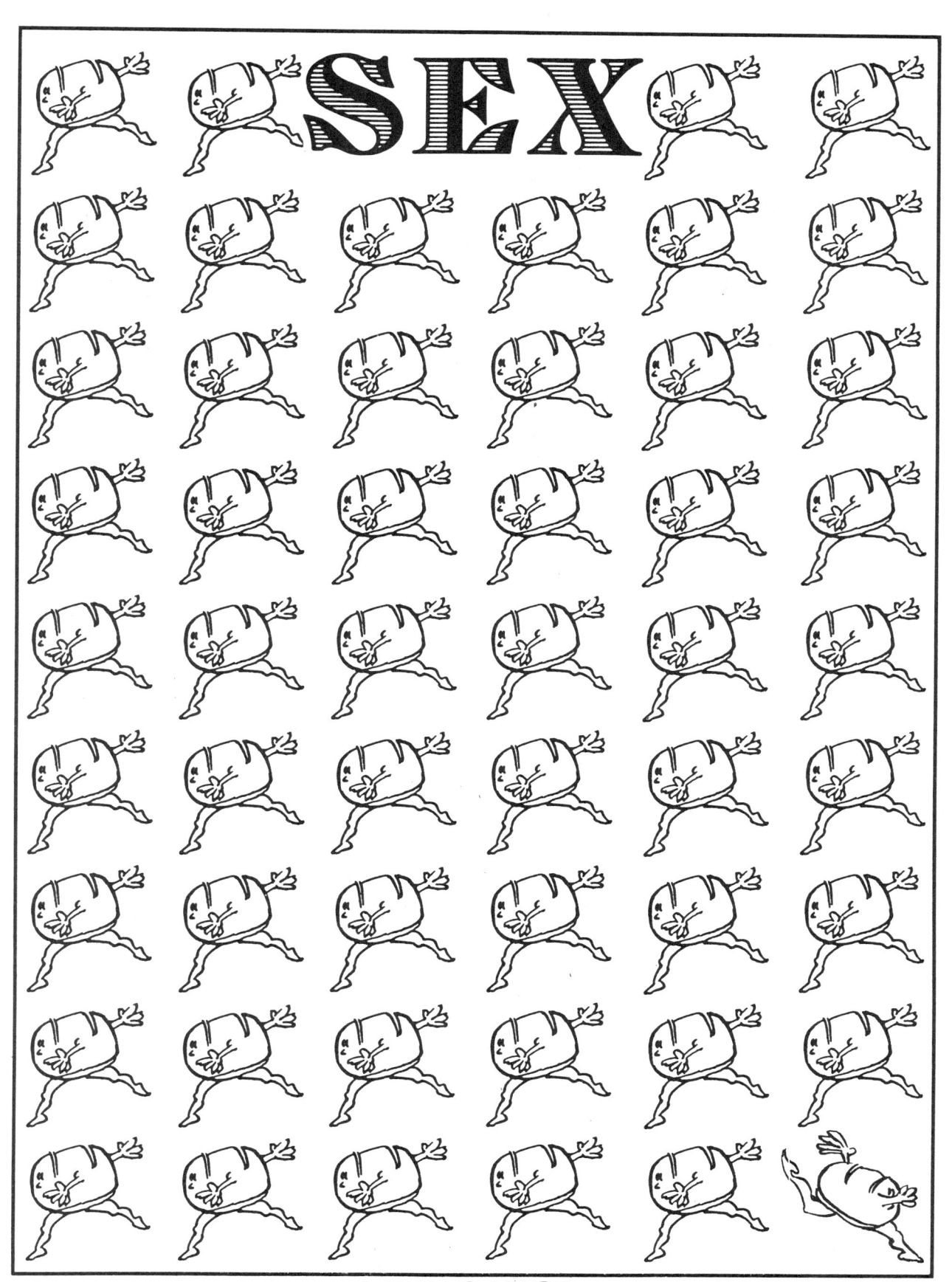

A BUN DANCE

Splurge

Indulge the urge to merge.

Animal/Cracker

Your animal will set you free.
Listen to it yearning mournful
in the night.

Dull not its passion with your structured lies.
You, conceived in thrusting locking of groins,
   thrutched from mother's body,
   living through breast lactating,
   a hunter moving through the thicket,
   driven to perpetuate yourself.

You, beneath your civilized refinements:
you, an impassioned human,
   Stalking hungry to survive, mate
                   kill
                   nest and
                   nurture.
Your fanciest mind cannot contain
the animal wild who bears your name.

Will sex with you be
inconsistent? or in consistent?
infrequent? or in frequent?

Mate

Hesitate:
Masturbate

Cooperate:
Copulate.
Procreate.
Perpetuate.
Consecrate.
Liberate.
For Heaven's
Sake.

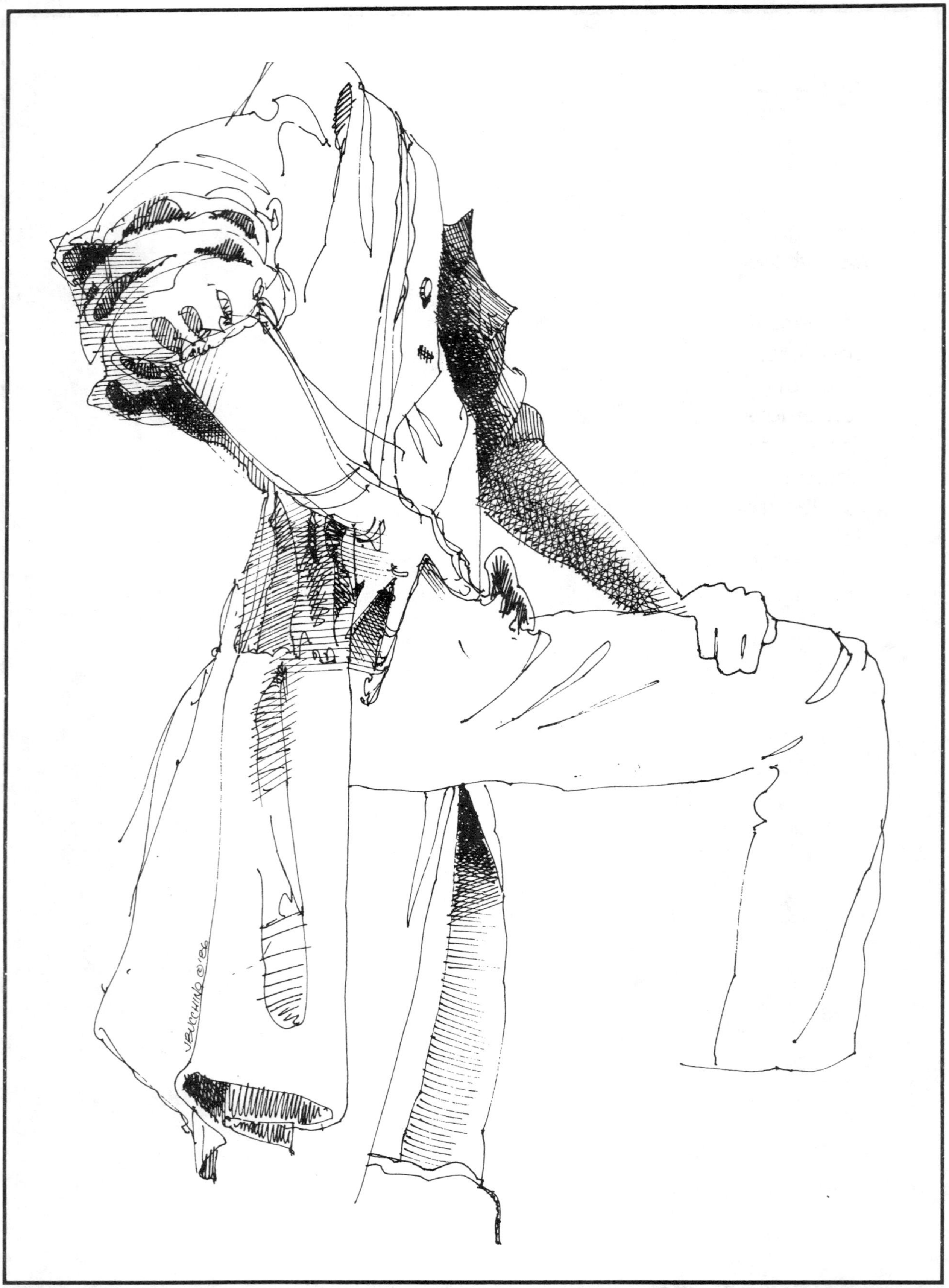

Gift

I will take you finely wrapped,
perfectly appointed in your trappings,
peeling off the garments slowly.
No three-piece suit, though modern armor,
will stop my tender most advances.

Penetrate-persistent I will loose
the would-be barriers;
bare your guarded secrets
and unleash you to your yearning.
As your breath sweeps you in fire
I will suck-hold your desire.

Fluid creaming and careening,
spacing in confusion.
Locked in thrusting tightly
in her, out her,
rigid mighty.

Once, you wandered in a desert;
now, your love has come upon you.
I (who knows your passion brewing)
Spinning liquid to forever.

I will take you in my valley
captured lusty by the hunger;
yielding to our power.

I will take you, you'll surrender.

Animal Man / Gentle Man

Tear and bite, rip and claw,
teasing tongue, pleasing awe.
Your silent lust; sprinkled by hesitancy,
unleashes my lust and hesitancy.

I am pulled into your soft eyes
lost In uncharted roads.
Your changing eyes: soft and hard,
               strong, scared,
               quizzical, knowing,
               fading in,
               reaching out,
pull and tear me
into love, lust and confusion.
I will bite you,
(rip and clawing)
hold you tightly to forever,
and caress you
(to your yearning).

I always liked M&M's:
That thin cracking shell
housing the milky chocolate
that melts in your mouth.

An-Atom-Me

Mouths;

    open caverns wet,
    lip-luscious visit
    to never-forget.

Eyes (speaking silent)

    connect at our core,
    giddy and dizzy,
    begging for more.

Our bodies;

    linked in ecstacy,
    freed by the genuine
    you,
    us and
    whee!

After Glow

Skimming clouds,
our plane silhouettes shadows big and little,
our tail leaves misty tunnels like
twirling mustaches.

Topping snow rich mountains,
our skis slice tracks exuberant,
our sunburn smiles dot the snow.

Your silent, sexy loving slides past
my secret boundaries;
illuminating corridors.

Radiant in our afterglow
I remain:
Elevated,
titillated,
satiated,

consecrated.

After Sex

I wanna tiss ue

Male Energy

You please me once and then again,
you seem tired, but just when
I think you are satiated
you knock, (unanticipated)
at the door of lover's leap
breathing hard, curling feet.

You wind me up to love for hours,
would you say I'm penis powered?

Come In

Your smiling penis
came a-knocking at my heart,
thrusting, throbbing in my
most sacred gentle secrets.

Your smiling penis
marched an army
of giggle plenty into my
elated body.

Your power/passion opens doors
to hidden treasure and
merriment resplendent.

My corridors echo in the
rhythm of your knocking.
Yes. Oh yes; come in!

Vide-Oh

See us on that screen
as we cleave onto one another
played back; our intertwining limbs
laced in lusty-love abundant.
Our clearly crystal image
baptized by this time distortion.

God's come home on your T.V. tube, my love
bringing us: Us in Living Color.
Light and man and woman;
baptized by our act of love reflected.

Ecstasy

You and me.

Orgy

A riot of elation
dancing wildly
through my sensors
giggle twirling
colors swirling
wild wind whipping.
To hell with sipping.

When?

When again will your lips, so tender, rest on mine?

When will I travel the lost worlds of your eyes?
And breathe your flesh and the faint softness of your smile?

And when again will I lay with you and feel us
so perfectly alive?

Fondle Of You

Lick and suck,
drip and pluck,
kiss me deep
my man.

Breathing hot,
alive what-not,
from your greatest fan.

Stroke and swell,
you can tell
our hearts pound
in unison.

Thrust and probe,
pulsing lobe,
begging juices
to explode.

Your sacred flesh
upon my flesh.
I'm hungry for your touch.

Come home to me.
Oh, can't you see,
you've been gone far too long.

A hand in the bush
is worth two birds afar.

ABSTINENCE MAKES THE HEART ~~GROW~~ *go wander* FONDER

I Met Your Wife Today

I met your wife today;
sweet of face,
warm of disposition.

I met your wife today;
friendly smiling,
exchanging pleasantries.

I met your wife today;
and she spoke her
name in greeting.

I like your wife;
Beautiful in every way.
Young firm women,
sisters, she and I.

And, when next I lie
upon her pillow,
and marvel at your maleness,
and the view;

I will hear my heart whisper
that I met your wife,
and that in a strangely tangled way,
I like your wife.

Impotence

Pend-u-lust

Purr Pet You Ate

My legs,
   love knots enfold you,
tied so I can't hold you.
You lick my hummer button,
none of me forgotten.
Rock hard, strong male figure,
plunging tongue and finger;

Nip and tease,
oh, God,
oh please,
no more, no more
and then again
notify my next of kin.

I swoon,
I melt,
I cream,
I moan.
Now it's OK;
you can leave me alone.

More Ass

"Sexually oriented?"
"No, horny bitch."
"Like I said:
Sexually oriented."

Sex Is F....d

Prostitute:
A good time had by all.

In The Pubic Domain

First herpes attack:
a foreign lesion.

I Am Not A Wind-Up Toy

I am not a wind-up toy
put here for your pleasure.

Inside this beautiful body
is a vulnerable heart
open and giving
with scar tissue
from folk like you
who forget
to notice me as human.

Behind this face,
blessed with female softness,
is a mind with eyes
that see your actions
louder than your voice.

I am not a wind-up toy
made by God to please some boy.
My vagina ain't a bag of tricks,
my hair ain't made of pick-up sticks.

I am human just like you
from my Clairol hair
to my Gucci shoes.

Photo by Jon Nicholas

When you get into sexual harrassment,
you get into a fuzzy area.

Udder Confusion

"I've been man-nipple-ated,"
she tittered.

Dating Game Reject

I woke up this morning and
there you was gone.
Your butts in the ashtray
but you left at dawn.

Oh, love 'em and leave 'em,
they're all the same.
You've hurt me real bad,
Mister what-was-your-name.

   I should have known better
   when I met you last night,
   but I just had my nails done
   and my bra was too tight.

   I should have sensed something
   when you said 'Howdy do,'
   spilled your martini,
   and tripped on my shoe.

I woke up this morning and
there you was gone.
Your butts in the ashtray
but you left at dawn.

Oh, love 'em and leave 'em,
they're all the same.
You've hurt me real bad,
Mister what-was-your-name.

'My you have muscular legs,'
you said,
'Now let's cut this small talk
and jump into bed.'

You was hairy and drunk,
and smelled pretty bad,
and I knew I could love you,
you're so much like my dad.

I woke up this morning and
there you was gone.
Your butts in the ashtray
but you left at dawn.

Oh, love 'em and leave 'em,
they're all the same.
You've hurt me real bad,
Mister what-was-your-name.

   You're a rotten imitation,
   a dirty, low-down fake.
   You stayed to lick my frosting
   and left and took the cake.

xxOO

Is There Life After Lust?

Moth to a flame
drawn by your name.
You like fast:
   bikes,
    skiing,
     women.
You totter on the edge of forbidden,
blatantly open,
silently hidden;
sex ready,
stoned heady,
blue eyes flashing,
tickle tongue lashing
sensitive,
warm,
kind
and loving.
You're on my mind
going and
coming.

Russian Caviar

Dark, rich, lusty male;
feelings the texture of brown bread.
Wrapped in the Earth's time warped mold.
Hold on to life, hold on to me . . .
We are one.

My Prince

My prince,
your magic wand
has awakened in me
my lost desire.

My longing had lain
abandoned in a long forgotten room,
when you,
cloaked in manhood,
ravaged the barriers from my soul,
the shields from my heart,
and opened me to your perfect love.

I swoon to the fierce mystery
of your eyes.

My timeless male.
My sweet samovar.

Virgin territory: No man's land.

• • • • • •

Chasity is its own punishment.

LOVE

4

MET A PHORE

Let
Out
Vital
Energy

I Love Me

I move myself to
the other side of
my resistance
with my non-judgmental
loving.

The jewel that I am
sparkles larger
than the polished stones of
my refinements.

Because in the radiance
of my sparkle
I reflect a galaxy of
stars for wishing,
and a flood of new skies.

I am the breeze I breathe.
With me I renew;
open, kind, and true,
loving, beautiful and free.

It's easy to love me.

Wedding Vow

Today, we are planting a seed in our garden.
We are honored to have family and friends,
standing at the border of that garden and
witnessing its unique beauty.

It took a long time in coming, this garden of ours.
With love and patience we carefully tilled the soil
by taking time to really talk to one another.
And listen. And hear.

Bravely, we removed, one by one,
the weeds of fear, self-deceptions, competition,
old hurts and loneliness;
and lovingly replaced them with understanding,
vulnerability, empathy, compromise and yielding.

And the sun came
and the rain
and small miracle rainbows!
Our garden dazzles my eyes
with its sparkling energy
and giddy colors!

So, today,
because we have both agreed
to care enough to act with
each other's best interests at heart
we are planting a new seed.

I love me,
I love you,
I love us.

It will grow to be the most beautiful
and precious flower of all
and will reign over all the rest.

The seed is trust
and we have lovingly planted it on this day.

Photo by Jon Nicholas

You Of My Dreams

The choice was made long ago.
The day my heart told me so.
You of my dreams,
you of my nights.
You bring me joy,
and peace,
and light.

Sometimes we hurt before we can feel.
Sometimes we pretend
before coming to real.

I don't want you to go away.
You belong next to me,
I want you to stay.

You linger on every breeze
and every breath I take.
You touch me fully,
my beautiful mate,
whether I'm asleep or awake.

Want: Add

Men want what women want what
men want women want what men
want women want what men want
women want what men want women
want what men want women want
what men want.

It Matters

In matters of the heart,
the heart speaks truth.
Only the mind is capable of deception.

In matters of the body,
the body speaks the purest tones.
whereas the mouth may lie.

In matters of the soul,
the spirit guides speak clearly,
(providing our fears will let us hear.)

In matters of you and me,
I have listened to my heart
and my body and my soul,
and they have answered simply:
Love.

Shopping Trip: You + Me = Us

In shopping for your life-last-love,
try on us.

Cloaked in us,
walk about your old patterned rooms.
Go to parties,
meetings
or your books.

Visit surgeons,
and in the harshest light,
dissect
the convoluted possibilities.

And if,
(after walking through the mirrored halls,
reflecting on the eyes of loving friends,)
you find we fit,

wear us home;

that is
if we become you.

Your Party

Your face changes to a parade of faces,
each different.
Your words fitting and not fitting
the faces you wear.
You flitter just beyond my solid
understanding:
Elusive as moonlight,
a holographic light show
pulsing gentle my senses.

You are a collage,
alive in full colored beauty.
I'm glad I could come to your party!

Spontaneous Combustion

Smokey the Bear warned me against
playing with matches in
restricted areas.
Prevents innocents getting burned.

Thinking of my heartfelt lover so far away,
your sparking eyes
and lusty softness
ignited my nervous system to a raging fire.

Startled by the flames
I run burning in the thicket.
"Only you can prevent forest fires,"
says the bear.

If I Were Clear

If I were clear,
and holding hands with God,
I would draw your essence to mine
in intoxicating space and
  grace.

If I were whole,
living from an open heart;
I would bathe your most timid fear
with full lovelight rare
  and care.

But I am newly on this path,
learning as I walk,
sticking to stagnant fossils
of the past
   that last.

If you feel me blur,
shielding walls within my
fractured heart,
think kindly of me as I go
   and know

Beneath this well-formed skin
remains your mate,
and if with patience you prevail,
you'll learn my love is true.
I will merge
   with you.

Gale

Jimbo Jumble,
hear the rumble
coming o'er the plain.
Once it catches up with you,
you'll never be the same.

Moving in a blurring gale,
too fast to leave a vapor trail.
With a power so immense,
you can't escape;
there's no defense.

I'm the love you've hungered for,
the one you've needed to adore,
a perfect match for all you do,
sent by God
to nurture you.

So yield to me, my precious one.
Your time for love has finally come.
We're thrust in life's pervasive flow,
with the deepest love
two souls can know.

Don't Inner Fear

We are victims only of our fear,
can't you hear? It's clear.
We don't let others near, out of fear.

You fear that I will go away
and you can't cope,
so you defend and pretend.

I fear the end is near,
so I do just like you,
pulling away, too.

Staring upon each side of our wall,
we wonder why we went away.

Forget your fear. I am here.

Love Talk?

Was it just love talk?

Flaming words in a moment of release?
As real at that moment as dreams are real?
Brush strokes painted in passion
and stroking fingers?

Was it just love talk?

You. Are you true?

Me. Can I see?

Us. Can we be?

Photo by Jon Nicholas

Heart Song

I feel your crazed heart
cracked by disappointment.
I feel your open heart
hunger for commitment.

My strong fingers cradle your
heart as a fragile down-duck,
and tuck it precious into my own heart.

Together in rhythmic harmony
we stroll and lull
in the meadow of our dawn.
We two melded as one:
so perfectly alive.

Melt

Melt: soft brown eyes,
hands silken on skin,
escalated breathing of our passion.

Creamed: words,
poems ringing joyous
in the silence.

Love: Puddles deep.

Forget the end.
Let me love you, my friend.

You Are A Part Of Me

You are a part of me when apart.
You are a way to my peace when away.
You are the end of all thoughts I start.
Softly I melt to your name on my heart.

I Want To Drift In Your Eyes

I want to drift in your eyes,
love away your heartache sighs,
wrap you in a candy box,
tickle your sweet goldy locks.

I'll dissolve the sadness of your
hollow disappointments.
I'll be mountains for you to conquer;
a brook to refresh;
a meadow to lie down.

I will be your healthy escape
as natural as each breath you take.
In your haunted silence
I will echo my love
like a bell.

I want you to drift in my eyes,
love away my heartache sighs,
and open up my tender box,
stacking love like building blocks.

I Awaken Still

Perhaps time will not allow
us space to walk deeper in our dream,
and you must depart to other worlds afar.

If this is so, if this must come to pass,
please know that in my yearning as you go:
My body remembers, my heart is open,
and I awaken still with your name
soft upon my lips.

Tonight

Tonight you are with me,
crowding my mind to the tiniest cranny.
Tonight your name surrounds me.

Darling maestro,
you strum my primal self
like a harp.
I resonate to your touch tender.
Our music, bigger than
the sky, climbing, intoxicated,
into forever.

Tonight I am yours.
Tonight you are mine.

Do You Remember?

On a wisp of scent carried in a silent breeze,
    do you remember me?
      Though your days are full with crowding of your plans,
    do our smells ever pay you a secret call?
    Or my name echo as a chime upon your ear?
And does your body,
in its quiet wisdom,
recall moments long ago when we so perfectly adjoined,
learned to fly above ourselves
while singing harmony with May?

I want to love you.
I want you to love me.
I want us to flourish.
I want us to be.

Deviant

There is dignity in staying in line:
adhering to structure and rules.
One gets much respect by singing along,
not varying the words or the tune.

Yet, I am taking a bigger risk
by refusing to compromise
the truth in my heart,
by pretending my life
and moving away from your eyes.

Stripped Naked

Stripped naked, we have risked
to stand before one another
   revealing convoluted secret self-talk:
      loves,
      lives,
      hopes,
      dreams.

We touch the vulnerable walls of our delusions
and feel them melting as they go.

Your earth eyes reveal my deepest fathoms lost.

Our love (bare and beautiful)
laughing colors
through our monochrome illusions.

Richly-risking rascals we,
grandly naked
in vulnerability.

Land Of Promises

I didn't know this could happen to me.
I didn't know I could feel so free
'til I dared venture the wilderness of your eyes
(veiled and revealed; perfectly alive).

I hadn't planned to find you
in this land of promises.

I didn't know that
soul love came in packages
real and breathing.

That my heart
(bruised and locked in loneliness)
   would open like fireworks
   on that day in July.

Then, my sweet and strongest male,
you found me,
answering my silent yearning
with your bold-toothed smile.

You are my knowing beyond words.
You are a river raging
through my dreams and nights.
Reflecting and growing,
moving in your flooding maleness,
I ride your currents.

Now, I know.

Communication

It's not where I end that you begin,
for we're both simply human under our skin.

We may sport a posture or play our own game,
but in truth we're all one, we're all one and the same.

Oh, our histories vary, the way we each wrote it;
pathetic, forgotten or sweet candy-coated.

We each spend our time in what we call our life.
We often feel separate or distant in strife.

But in fact we're united. We are joined to the core.
Let us share our gut feelings.
That's what we're here for.

Photo by Jon Nicholas

Motorcycle Mama

Screaming silver bullet,
flashing snippets of road.
Dazzle-dangle images
plastered and gone.

Gauges reflecting sun and trees.
Others pass
waving the fraternal greeting of road bikers.
I cling, simian,
straddled upon your padded seat,
legs vibrating your engine.

Behind your helmet
(which keeps your softest lips
from mine)
I see the reddened crease
of your tender neck.
Your silken hairs spark golden
from your muscled arms
and windwhip your shirtsleeves.

Silenced in the droning,
I am lost to each of
those smallest, most silken hairs,
as we thrust into
a moving picture
catching glimpses of
forever and gone.

My love,
keep your green light showing
and we will ride
giddy and vibrating,
in a moving dance
filling our nows richly
into tomorrow and gone.

Trail Blazed Her

Lost my Dad;
was sad.
Lost my hymen;
was glad.
Lost a love;
the cad.
Lost my youth;
not bad.

Then I lost my way;

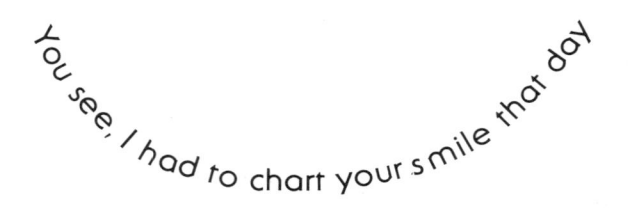

You see, I had to chart your smile that day

I had to travel by your map,
journey to your eyes;
navigated by your hands,
the softness of your sighs.

This exploration
(to the ragged valley of my soul)
leaves me lost;
makes me whole.

Journey

Perfectly flawed,
I am captured in the
hidden valley of your textured asymmetry.
Waves of fluid emotion
have brought never-ending
faces that you wear.

As you chart your predetermined course.
(Searching for the treasure of your elusive dreams)
I listen to the purity of your boyish candidness,
marvel at the tenderness of your healing heart
and ride the excitement of your fire lust.

The journey to the land of your soul
is my journey.

We are one.

East Coast

Bubble bathing blue,
sailing home to you.
Warm and heavy depth,
melting intermeshed with
fragments lacing doubt.
What are we about?

Then I calm upon your chest,
softly I'm at rest.

Sweetest heart,
when I touch
your creeping memory
(stealthy through the silence
of my drifting fog),
I know we are the harbor
of all light.

Right on course;
I will sail to port,

an open vessel
filling with love beams.

Can't Wait

I contemplate:
fate,
my mate,
a tête a tête,
great elate!

Shejonny

Shejonny, Shesweety,
succulent, meaty,
I dream of you baby.

Logic? Obsession?
Real? Or just guessin'?

My body remembers
our hearty romance,
our joyful love dance.

I miss you, Dear, for
you have touched me,
you have reached me,
deeply, completely.

Love and light:
 chuckleworthy ,
your beauty leaves me
topsy turvy.

Bloomin'

As real as springtime's
newest daisy,
you blossom me
to wacko crazy.

Charming / Disarming

Stoned sober.
Hooked in snatch;
foggy patch
love addiction;
bondage tie
locked by your
blue binding eyes.

You've got me hot and needing you.
You influence the things I do.
Please don't pull your love from me;
I'm full and alive in our energy.

En-tranced

Hypnosis in its truest form;
my furry thoughts, my face so warm.

As in a trance I follow you.
What you suggest is what I do.

Your magic wand strokes me so deep,
my words are lost, I cannot speak.
My attention rivets
on your hands
as you conduct my one-man band.

All rational thoughts are left behind.
I guess it's true that love is blind.

I Want To Do You In

Sometimes I want to do you in,
and then you flash your boyish grin.
I think that you, I should delete,
and then you mutter, smiling; "squeat.*"

I wish I knew how you disarm;
you wrap me helpless with your charm.
You chide, provoke and then seduce,
my power's but a poor excuse.

You have me packaged, wrapped and tied;
a present tense, and hypnotized.
You twist me round your little digit,
ain't you 'shamed you silly nidget?

* squeat = let's go eat

Poem

Last night,
   wrapped in sensuality,
heady with smell and taste,
you asked me to write you a poem.

Your crystal eyes: probe/glistening.
Your gentle voice: strokes/listening.
Your maleness enveloping.
Like a metronome, your heart,
rhythmically marks timeless time.

Paced, metered and flawless,
you carry me to ecstacy.

My love, you are a poem
and I am lost for words.

For You

For you I risk.
For you I trust.
For you I give.
For you I must.

With you I renew.
With you I share.
With you I joy
and fully care.

I want you to be all
that you aspire.
I want to elevate you even higher.
I want to dwell within your dreams.
I want our truth to remain as it seems.

Crystal

Magic from Earth's bosom
shines sunlight into shooting stars.
Powerful,
hypnotizing,
healing,
subtle.
Simple,
complicated,
clear,
hiding a glorious rainbow.

A multifaceted gem:
Blaring magnificent
in darkness.

Like you.

Concert of Jon

Titillating treble,
gorgeous trouble,
rhythm sections
pounding, probing,
pudding sections.

Mush band,
orchestrated
beyond the muzak.
We know the score,
Jon is in concert,
the room rounding rich
in his rolling thunder
and gentle giggles.

Heartland

With you, the world
is a warm heart
embracing us in rhythm.

All loves gone before, in all of time,
have known this joyous heartland.
Now, here we are, embraced in rhythm,
bathed in sunlight,
holding hands with Spring.

Merged and Melded

Merged and melded,
open ended,
old hurts mended:
bliss transcended.

Playmate

Playmate,
when we venture out
(you the fearless leader;
I your loyal scout),
the world is fat and bold with mornings
and sunshine and flower smells.

Playmate,
when we laugh,
the clouds shiver silver in delight
and the earth stops golden in our shiny eyes.

And, Playmate,
when we're wrapped, limbs entwined
(man and woman lost in time),
we know life's meaning greater than philosophers
combined.

Playmate,
even in silence,
our love is spoken.
If only we chose to listen.

In harmony we come to resolution.

You Are A Joy!

A joy you are!
Your shiny pleasures surge
my brain, like Pachinko balls.

Aglow, in our afterglow,
I radiate fire that you
(so skillfully) reignite, fan, and stoke.

Morsels of your smell,
              teeth,
              hair,
              laugh,
              dewy eyes,
              silken secret places,
              and your throaty moaning in the night,
flicker file behind my eyes.

My path is lighted by your name.
Glowing,
I reflect our time together,
as darkened alleys flood with sunlight
   one by one.

You never remember my name,
but I'm glad to love you
just the same.

Holy-Day

That slick brochure,
gushing in full color ink
(Marriott's finest),
can't come close to you.

Your chest is an island
capturing my dreams.
Your eyes, the bluest
of tropical nights.
Your arms,
majestic mountains,
holding me fast.

My darling, precious love,
we will winter in the quiet wood,
summer by a bed of brooks
and roll past the turning leaves
on a slope of babies' tears.

I Have Been Loved By You

I have been loved by you
to the bottom of my tendermost follicles.
I have been loved by you
deeper and more profoundly than spring.
I have been loved;
dumb-struck in your silent avalanche
and lust.
Your love visits
the hidden cul-de-sac of my dreams.
I have been loved by you.
You have touched me.

My cat is feline fine.

Banking On Us

A matter of
principle for you
and
a matter of
interest for me.

Ha R Money

MOM, DAD, & APPLE PIE

TOAD IN

Nostalgia is not what it used to be.

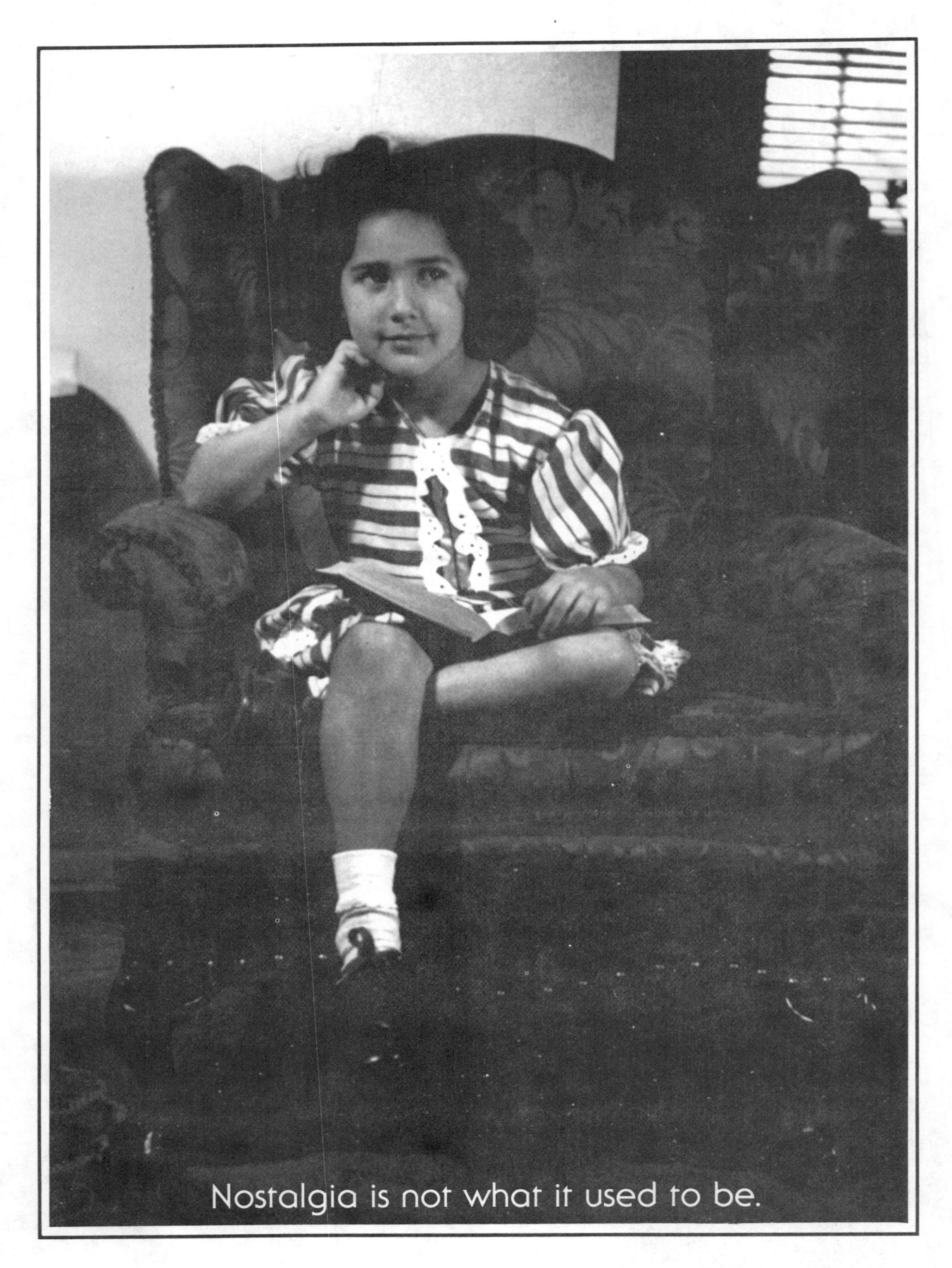

My Prized Possession

My prized possession when
I was a kid was a
rattlesnake's rattle.
Parched translucent by the sun.
I would shake it and in its
brittle hallowness I could
trace sliding patterns in
far away sand.

My hopes then were grainy wisps;
Dreamed paths that I would
trace as I left the hollow
prison of my childhood;
in search of dreams.

I would marry and merge with
a Roy Rogers daddy-boy
and together, Roy and Dale,
we'd cross the purple prairie
growing fat on ice cream,
babies and giggles.

We'd dine along the way
with presidents, Mickey Mouse,
and our kindergarten teacher.
Daddy'd tuck us in at night
after singing at starry campfires.

And sometimes, while swinging in a hammock,
I would talk to God.
And that's how it was for me.

I often wonder where
my rattlesnake rattle got off to:
Discarded in a cardboard box full of
old papers and rocks and feathers, perhaps,
slithered soft through sands of time;
leaving sliding patterns
and a brittle sound behind.

Photo by John Bruecker

South High Class of '62

Hodad, surfer, creep, or jock:
All were categorized.
Where you ate lunch and with whom;
your ranking had no disguise.

Surfer girls had bubble do's,
teased and hair sprayed tight,
tennies, with matching socks,
and slumber parties at night.

Huarached surfers, with lemon-bleached hair,
(no longer than their collars),
church-keyed beer in their woodies.
"Bitchen!" they would holler.

Hodads had that vaseline shine,
homamas in beehive ratting,
smoked in the head (so it was said),
and rarely were seen chatting.

Honor society eggheads
joined Order of Apollo or Athena,
policed the traffic, enforced the rules,
and kept the campus cleaner.

God help you if you were a creep.
Might as well lay down and die.
And no matter how others labelled you,
each feared the creep was "I."

(continued)

Mr. Rowe taught "Freshman Problems,"
in a sweltering quonset hut space.
My problem was how to be popular
without attending a "submarine race."

Wearing socks on our new gym floor
at a dance called the "Howdy Hop,"
to the Everly Brothers, we Lindied and Strolled,
to The Big Bopper, we did the Bop.

"Off the grass," "Where's your hall pass?"
"Don't step on the senior lawn.
They'll throw you in the trash can,
and that's where you belong."

Hershey and Barr were teachers,
and some names of other proctors:
Gutter, Butts, Ball, Bunyan,
Misters Barbar, Farmer, and Dokter.

For four years, we persisted,
learned an alma mater few could sing,
and, many pimples later,
we wore our senior ring.

Now I'm in my forties,
and I pluck out my white hair,
and think fondly of South High School,
and how I grew up there.

Dirty Laundry

When I turned 40,
time inversed
back to the time I felt the worst.
Paralyzed in a quiet collision
of rules, diversion, indecisions.
My life wasn't happy any more.
No matter how I shut the door,
my childhood pains spread like cancer
pushing that door, demanding I answer.

So, I chose to be taller than my defenses
regardless of the consequences.
If I stayed trapped in family lies
I might as well lay down and die.
So this is how it really was;
straight from the fist,
not from the glove:

"It must be a girl," Mom screamed at my birth.
She had her game to play
and a baby girl, all plump and round,
fit in her scheme some way.
I was the doll to live her drama
of little sister, big bad brother,
love and hate, compete with father,
and her own abuse from Dad and Mother.

Dad fed her chocolates to keep her fat
so he justified his lover
and working late, he left us home
to be cared for by our mother.
His buddy, Barney, the pharmacist
kept her stocked in diet pills
which she drank with pots of coffee
to add more caffeine thrills.

(Continued)

For six or seven hours she would scream out words of hate:
"I don't deserve you stupid kids. You're mean. Oh, what a fate."
She'd hold me down, rubbing raw, my "filthy" female parts
and told her friends, with dewy eye, that I was her sweetheart.
She stuffed down cake and ice cream
and slept with sleeping pills.
My dad worked late at the office so he could pay the bills.

My brother tortured bugs and ants
and threatened me with no second chance.
Our house was a box with holes punched in it.
Life was a contest: no way to win it.
The sky was mom's scream-ramble-talk around my ears and eyes
as everything I experienced, she interpreted and analyzed.
"Pretend to do what your husband says...love is a competition."
"Manipulate and get your way; control all the decisions."

I learned to please with a passive grin as Mom's voice reverbed
in my head.
Until I turned 40 and paralyzed in pain and nearly half dead.
If you're saying "Get off it; that was then."
"Why turn 40 and live it again?"
Perhaps, you're not caught in self-denial, or have another cure
or maybe you were fortunate, or maybe you're not sure.
As for me: ignoring pain, caused my pain to stay
and when I fully felt my hurt
the pain it went away.

That was then and now I'm free,
honest,
liberated.
I love myself,
forgive the past,
and I am
consecrated.

I Learned Early

I learned early not to fight the big woman
   as she bellowed up and down the hall,
   hollering, wailing.

I learned to stand silent in my closet
   trying to pretend she was just a shrill foghorn
   in an ocean far away.

I learned, before I can remember knowing how
   to learn, to smooth the fury with humility
   and be the ideal little girl.

I learned early to court the big man with
   total idolatry, and do it perfectly so I'd
   never feel the strap and his bulging eyes
   like my brother who dared fight back.

Control was destined to be my Olympic event.
   I went into training.
   I practiced anytime I heard someone in the house.
   Anytime I met someone new.
   Anytime.

By eight I had perfected the performance.
   My feelings and bowels were totally impacted.
   "Good nature" and "easy going"
were gold medal material.

   And, somewhere in my intensive training,
   I slipped away from myself
   as silently as a marshmallow
   into a cup of hot chocolate.

The Best She Could

She had done the best she could.
With what she had she'd done real good.
Held back in joy and stuck in pain
she did what she could to keep her sane.

She followed the rules as she understood them,
exercised options as she construed them,
gave her kids what she never had:
love and lessons. A house. A dad.

Her youth was a nightmare chasing a dream
wrapped around a primal scream.
She disguised all this in her perfect show,
hoping no one would ever know.

But we know:
She had done the best she could.
With what she had she'd done real good.

Daddy Died

Daddy died again tonight.
Buried long ago.
Daddy wrenched my guts from me
while I watched your show.

I remembered his eyes by looking at you.
I remembered his smell and his touch.
I pledged my allegiance to him once again,
and that energy scared you too much.

Perhaps, I never saw the man that you really are,
I only felt a broken heart heavy with his scar.
So fare thee well my daddy-lover,
tonight there's no denying;
you walked out and daddy's gone;
but it's me that's really dying!

Ghost

The ghost of your daddy
fills tonight like cobwebs.

When your were a boy-blossom budding,
your daddy prodded and cajoled you.
You were never enough to focus
his distorted soured vision.
And you,
flooded in fear and disappointment,
learned to go numb,
silent and sullen (avoid);
your mouth tacked down in pain.

Tonight:
fighting monsters of addictions
and loneliness,
you have returned —
budding silent and sullen,
your mouth and heart tacked down in pain.
You hallucinate your daddy as me
or you as your daddy.

Damn your daddy man.
He shouldn't be given a ghost of a chance.

Heavy

Some who diet lose their weigh,
then find it again another day.

Flattery

Tummy tuck.

Fat Joke

Fun at someone elses expanse.

Thanksgiving
(We can't go on eating like this)

Turkey, ham,
candied yams,
Cranberry sauce,
buns hot and crossed.
Pumpkin, mince, raisin pie,
mashed potatoes, mud in your eye.

Uncle Benny,
your cousin's new baby,
corn bread stuffing
with giblet gravy.
Clean your plate:
it'll go to waste
(the waist, of course, was mine).
"Seconds niece, pass the cheese."
"One small helping if you please."
Chew and swallow, I'm gonna burst.
I'll take some tea; I've such a thirst.

I'm stuffed and bloated like a fattened bird
(Alka Seltzer's a pleasant word).

I love to be in our family group
and mark the passing of our time,
as we give thanks for blessings all
and share this food and wine.
We've chewed the fat,
you're all so dear,
I'm grateful Thanksgiving's just once a year.

Fast food is the stuff that runs away from you.

Bletch

Sparkle, sparklie
twinkle cake,
I have got a belly ache
from candy, pie and
frosted flakes
instead of food
for goodness' sake.

My Mom Was Fat

My mom was fat.
She'd hide her flabby belly
in corsets and flowered muu-muus
and fly around,
jet propelled,
on diet pills.

At night,
pumping ice cream heaps in her ori-face;
like high speed trains through a tunnel:
She sat alone at the kitchen table.
The house creaked.
My father snored loudly in the bed,
and the cat stalked the night yard.

My mom was fat,
no doubt about that.

Think About Lipstick

Think about lipstick:
cream color paints.
Think about lipstick.
The beautiful model
puffed and buffed
seducing you to
think about lipstick
and callogen and liposomes,
autumn eyes,
perfumed thighs.
It's the "Avon calling"
dream.

A gurgle luscious stream.
Think about lipstick:
juicy kisses on
a lonely night.

Looking Good

That I spend time to look good and appeal to men
isn't because that's all I have to offer.
It's because I like being told I'm desirable.
I like feeling pretty.
I like seeing each toenail painted
and the softness of long hair down my back.
I feel feminine, lusty;
a soft cupcake good enough to eat.

I like the sparkle energy
men send my way;
hungry for cupcakes,
quietly window shopping with their eyes.

Shopping Mall Cruiser

As you cruise the shopping mall
your life force stops in a hovering stall.

You ponder the clothes that you could wear
to make the ladies stop and stare.

You buy the scent to drive them mad,
designer class, not some cheap fad.

You comb each store and look at stuff
marketed, packaged, displayed and such.

You strip the ladies with your eyes;
shopping bags serve as your disguise.

You've lived the dream you were taught to know;
your stuff is proof that you can show
that you're a success, that your life's no lie.

I pray your life force won't wither and die.

Hoarding Your Money

Miser y

Loose Change

Loose change
rattling out of our pockets;
out of our soil.

Loose souls
rootless,
looking for nourishment
and meaning in their seemingly aimless lives of
quests
and non-quests.

   Dave:
   Middle-aged, skin loosed around pinked nipples. Divorced,
   lonely, relocating "again." Looking backward while talking
   about forward. Carrying a hand mirror.

People;
strewn leaves upon our deserts,
beaches,
farmlands,
drifting in a hollow hope of an
unknown dream.

   Das Magnus:
   His pen name of course . . .
   (author of the yet unpublished River of Truth,
   hitchhiking in a 110° desert. "Love is equalibrium, with no
   ties or obligations. I don't need anyone. Look me up; how do
   I contact you?")

Loose change rattling out of our pockets:
Out of our soil.
Out of our hearts.

You Are A Turtle

You take your home where you go.
Self-contained in sun, rain, snow.
Throttle ready parked and steady.

If you didn't move in your abode,
I would title this poem "You are a toad."

Recreational Vehicle

we   R
heav   V

R.V. Resort Sales Presentation

The young scrubbed salesman will sell you your dream.

You made a promise; remember?

"I am going to travel when I retire. Pack up the wife, the dog
and the R.V. No boss. No clocks. Just relax, fish and follow
white lines across stretches of forever."

The bronzed salesman (born and raised in the next town) smiles.

"For just $5,000 the first year and $1 a night (no more than 7
nights in a row, or 2 visits a year in the same park. Annual fees
subject to change, of course,) you can stay in our resort. After
you join, if you recommend three other new members, you'll win a
free trip to Hawaii. Call ahead for reservations: sometimes we
run out of parking spots."

Tupperware, time-share,
Amway, Mary Kay
and pyramid schemes:
the salesman is paid to market your dream.

Be a window, not a blind
with no reservations;
pay him no mind.

Dam

This river is harnessed,
tethered by dams.
A wild horse broken by "flood
control."

Restrained from carving and
gorging grand canyons
in its raging wake.

This river is tethered.
Its primal force turning machines.

I flick my light switch and meet
the tamed river.

115° In The Shade

Relentless sun:
wool blanket face;
squint dry eyes.
Two fat boys sitting on the back
of each eyeball.
Shoulders seared red.
Nostrils parched into Sahara tunnels.
Brain: bran-caked; dry and dull.

The hot house tourists root to the
rocks with
lawn chairs and fishing lines.

Hell-hole hot
affordable lots.

Zion National Park

Sheer beauty,
   slices of red rock,
seduced by gravity,
stripped in sheets
striated and crusty.
Taken for granite.

Yonkers

Yonkers is bonkers
methinks.
L.A. is smoggy
and stinks.
Noise, fumes and slime
(sprinkled with crime)
are pushing me close to the brink.

Vegas

Dazzle flash.
Count your cash.
Smile for pay.
Come my way.
Money speaks
in greedy lust.
Ass and belly.
Suck a bust.

Sedona, Arizona

Sedona, Arizona
you've got that mellow tona
that makes me cruise and zona.

Art peeks from every pore:
red chunk mountains,
velvet skies,
rivers, rocks,
the moon: a crooked yellow smile.

Clop, clop, clop,
we ride in a surrey
with a fringe on top.
Native Americans,
tourists,
they all came,
cowboys and lovers,
drawn by your name.

Sedona, Arizona,
you've made me feel at homa.

Big Sur

The Big Sur is a princess
adorned in lacy white caps and kelp.
Her majestic breasts are shawled
in scattered rocks; embroidered with
sea lions and whales.
Hummingbirds kiss her misty hair
and flowers are her underwear.

Stars sparkle in her eyes;
water falls, tears in case she cries.
Her lashes are the redwood trees;
her royal blood, the surging sea.

Highway 1 is a ribbon looping,
the cars are enameled beads,
and we are seeds in the shadows
that her highness rarely sees.

The sun is her radiance,
the wind her breath,
clouds are pillows for
royal rest.

Pristine, private,
untamed power...
the Big Sur is a lady
at any hour.

Photo by Jon Nicholas

Stewardess Song

We're the girls in panty hose
and regulation scarf-tied bows;
working's our priority,
God, grant us our seniority.

    "Where will you work?"
    "Oh, I don't care."
    "Front or back?"
    "Just anywhere."
    "I'll slam the ovens,
    you exercise,
    I'll do the cooking,
    you apologize."

We're the girls in uniform,
frequent flyer battle-worn;
smiling's our priority,
God, grant us our seniority.

    Carry-on luggage,
    unaccompanied child,
    the guy in 4D
    drives me wild!
    It's not our fault;
    air traffic delay;
    put your cup
    upon my tray.

We're the ones who smell like Boeing,
with varicosic veins ashowing;
travel's our priority,
God, grant us our seniority.

(continued)

Kick a carrier, pop a cork,
pry it open with a fork.

>   Ice in the oven,
>   glue your nail.
>   The limo driver
>   might tell tales.

We're the girls all dream to be,
even though we're 53;
service is priority,
God, grant us our seniority.

>   Dry on the curtain,
>   give the ice a smack,
>   send the extra
>   to the back.
>   Cut him off,
>   that drunken toad!
>   He can't have another
>   "for the road."

We're the girls with suitcase wheelies,
muscles strong, "come here and feel these."
Life is our priority,
God, grant us our seniority.

>   Blame commissary;
>   our fault it's not;
>   did you see
>   the ring I got?
>   My man is gonna
>   marry me
>   because he wants
>   to fly free.

Yes, we're your stewardesses
on this ride.
In our job we have much pride,
you are our priority,
God, grant us our seniority.

Yule Survive

The cat ate the tinsel.
Our sink just broke.
Uncle Benny's had a stroke.

Not enough money
or enough time.
Salvation Army,
can you spare a dime?

Holiday cards from total strangers,
the Douglas fir could be endangerd.

Merchandizing, advertising;
What to buy you? I'm agonizing.

Who gets the kids for the vacation?
On Saturday night we have 6 invitations!
Christmas or Chanuka,
mixing traditions,
throwing Aunt Bertha into conniptions.

This is the season of holiday cheer
to share with those whom we hold dear.
A spiritual time for love and giving,
optimism and the joy of living.

So let tension and pressure,
in direct translation,
equal excitement and jubilation.

Happy holiday.
My love to you!
In all you are.
In all you do.

Rubber Babies

Bouncing babies
are an undulating mess
of rubber neck,
holes on their heads,
leaking from the ends
who look at us
like we're weird.

Some Fluffy Girl

Soon some fluffy girl will look your way
and you'll move on;
gone.

It seems that we just met, boy.
They placed you,
brand spanking new,
on my swelled belly.
"Hello," I said to those alert green eyes.
I'll teach lessons I may not have learned
before we say goodbye.

I was branded harsh in my tender years
left fighting demons of tears and fears.
We are all branded,
caught in lessons when we're young, son.
They stay long and make us strong.

I stroke your silken belly
and tickle your neck
and I won't forget
when your ship leaves my shore
to love you more.

Soon some fluffy girl will take you on her tide.
Have a lovely ride!

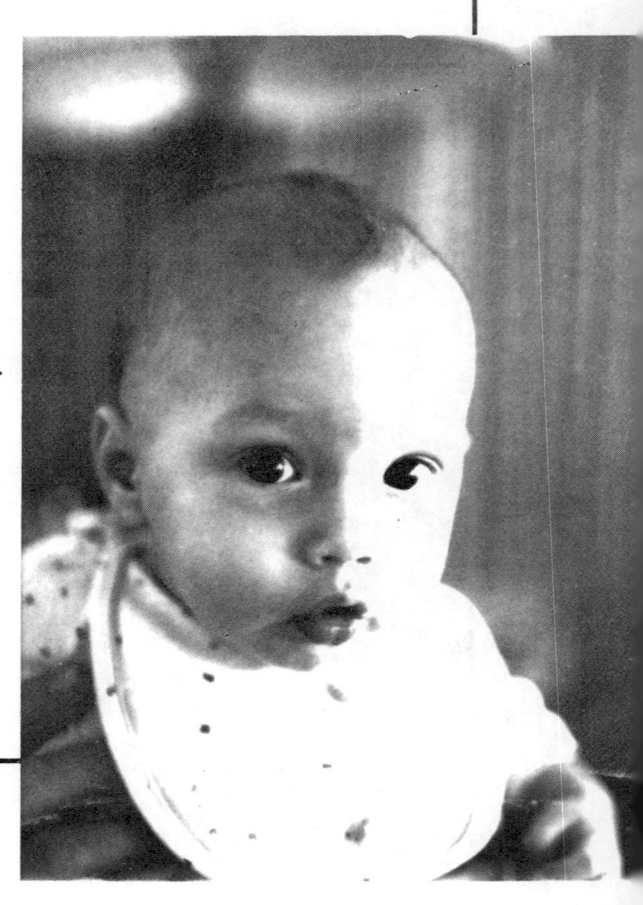

Setting Son: Rising Son

Such a fleeting time,
nubile son of mine.
Tender your hairless cheeks,
adult and little teeth chewing harmony with spring.
Skinny stretches of arms and legs,
a baby belly gone flat.
A man peeking through child eyes.

I watch you blooming son and your fragrance teases past me.
Your childhood will be a breeze on a warm day:
a scent you'll almost never forget.

Dear son of mine,
you are a jewel in my hallway of time.

Little Man

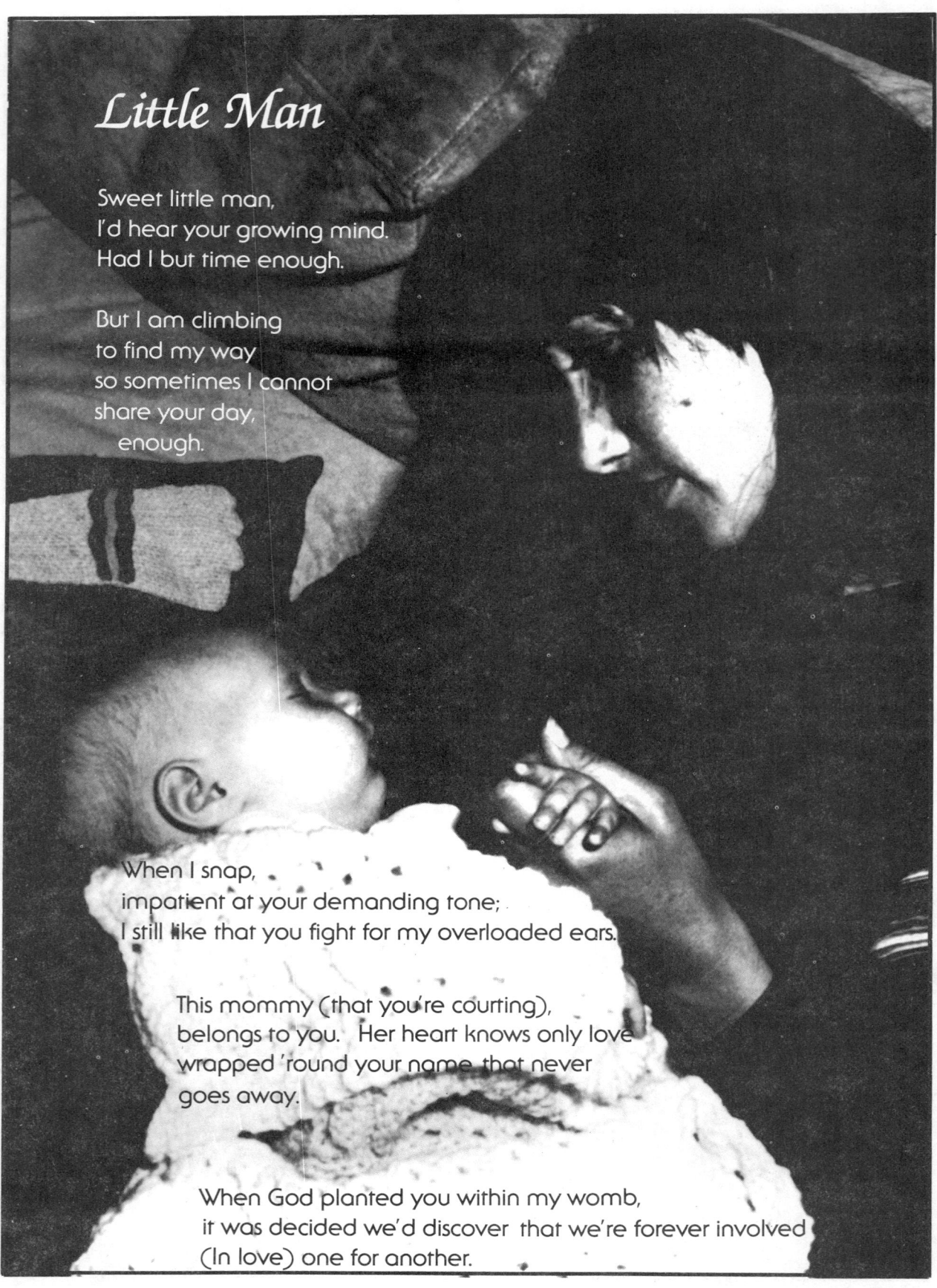

Sweet little man,
I'd hear your growing mind.
Had I but time enough.

But I am climbing
to find my way
so sometimes I cannot
share your day,
 enough.

When I snap,
 impatient at your demanding tone;
 I still like that you fight for my overloaded ears.

 This mommy (that you're courting),
 belongs to you.   Her heart knows only love
 wrapped 'round your name that never
 goes away.

 When God planted you within my womb,
  it was decided we'd discover that we're forever involved
  (In love) one for another.

Photo by Dennis Briskin

Bryce

Bryce, you are bright!
Your darkest of mostly green eyes
speaking in sparkles.
Wisdom and truth peeking at me.

I like the way you
think,
question,
play
and explore.
If I am critical,
it is myself that I abhor.

Bryce, I pray that not one day
slips away that I don't say:
"Bryce, you are beautiful."

My boy
stand tall,
for this mommy
you are perfect: all.

Single motherhood is a miss conception.

Tears
(By Bryce Stockwell, age 4)

Tears are water of islands salty with sea,
washing my pain to the outside of me.

A Minicure
(By Bryce Stockwell, age 5)

"It's so small it's less than a minicure."
A minicure is a oneth of an inch.
You see, if you cut an inch into
lots of little pieces and take 1000
in your hand: that's a 1000th of
an inch.
And if you pick one up: that's a oneth
of an inch.

There's nothing smaller than a minicure.

Neighbor

There's a shadow who lives next door.
Her name is Mary.

Fifty years ago she wrapped herself up
in a blanket and
left herself
on her children's doorstep.

I shot a smiling love beam at her
and she presented a graphic display
of her sons
   the 'Doctors'

I saw her again today
and she's still not home.

Last Night

(By Irving M. Lessin - 1934)

Last night,
after I thought of you,
I read a poem.

From an old and faded volume,
on a page by chance arrived at,
lifeless words,
long unlooked upon
lay before me.

Listlessly I read a line
and my mind at once awakened
as the dead words
stood out sharper,
sharper, bolder, clearer focused
on the page of yellowed paper.

Then I felt a burning fever,
a burning, scorching, blistering fever
engulf my mind and brain;
the dead words quivered on the page
and left its old and yellowed prison,
and spiralled up into my eyes
and entered on my brain.

It seemed so very strange to see
a blank yellow page in front of me,
and the words I just had read
were animated in my head.

On the blank yellow page in front of me
I saw what the words were meant to be:
A lover's heart that lives forever
took image on the yellowed paper.

Last night,
after I thought of you,
I read a poem.

FRIENDS & FOES

A PIER'S OUT OF NOWHERE

It's nice to be among friends,
even when they're not yours.

Photo by Jon Nicholas

31 Flavors

An ice cream scoop piled
those sundae mountains,
dripping in marshmallow fluff and
sauced with sky,
as we
(warm and dry)
crunch the road like nuts
feasting with our eyes.

Your smile
(and the sun)
dangle like a cherry on top.

Give It A Whirl

I am a stack of 45's
varied in rhythm and tempo.
Some blank for future recording sessions.
Each disk atuned in harmony; with me.

And you are a stack of 45's too.
It's true.
So why not come and play with me,
be-bopping syncopation?
Together we will harmonize
a giddy celebration!

Photo by Jon Nicholas

Your Beat

I used to pass much time
making reason
of your rhyme.

Before I understood
that it can't be understood.

The marching of your beat
speaks only to your feet.
And to try to mark your time
is beyond my frame of mind.

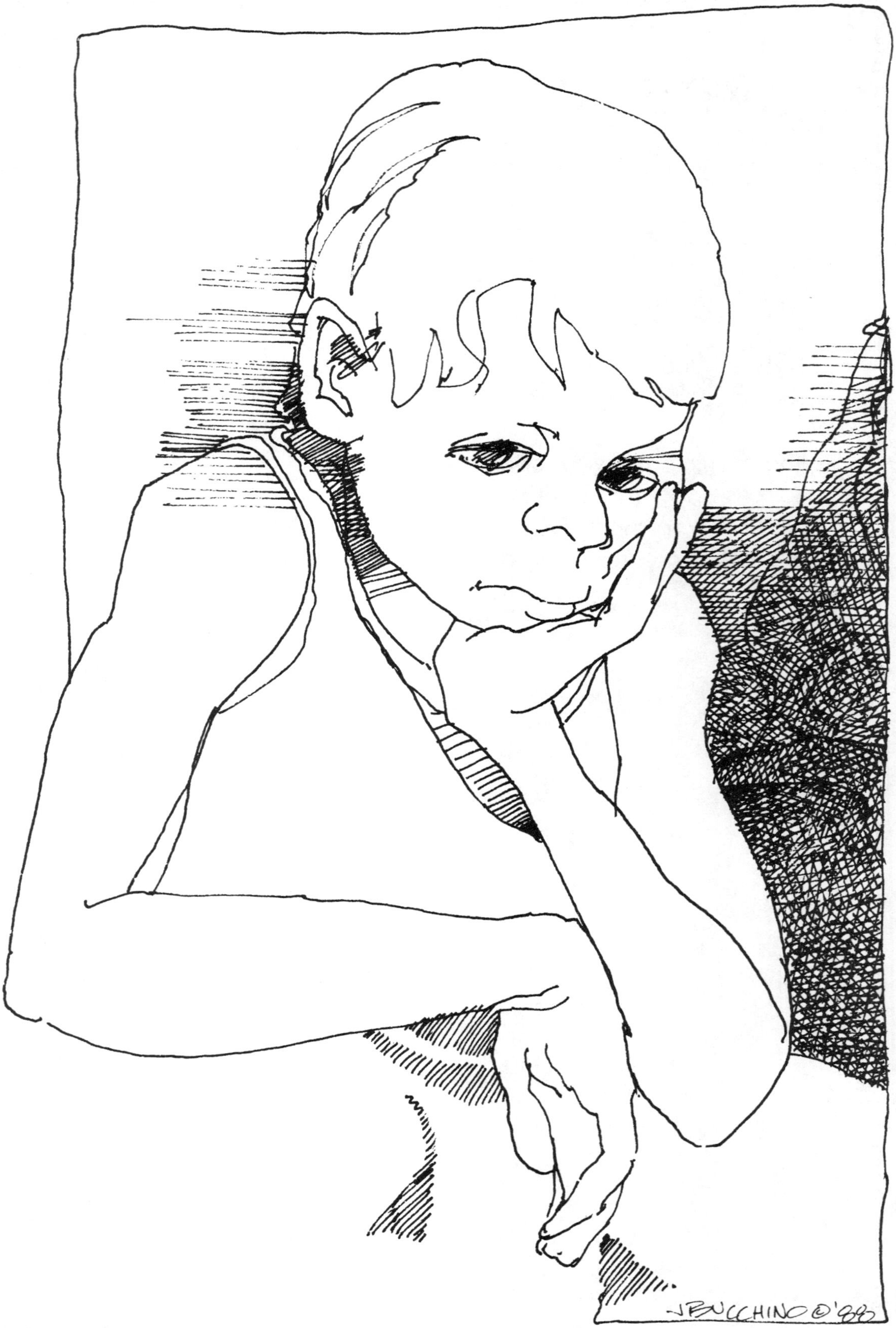
J BUCCHINO ©

Child

It's OK to be a child tonight, my love;
weak and tired in my arms.

Too weary to hold up your head,
be the way you feel, my love,
let it go;
give way to your tears!
The enemy's gone
and I am here
   to muss your hair,
   to stroke your skin,
   and hold you close against
   my breasts.

It's OK to be a child tonight, my love.

   No battles to win or worlds to conquer,
not strong or powerful.
Let go your pain,
the enemy's gone
and only I remain
   to hold you
   and fondle you
   and love you like a child.

It's OK to be a child tonight, my love.

   I already know the man,
   you scream him so,
   and drive him so.
Don't hide the child from me,
   let him appear, in my arms,
     without fear.

Bring your child to me,
let me hold him near.

Who?

Fogging in or fading out.
Silent thoughts or blaring shout.
Focused down; to hold that line
or misted, obscure; can't define.

I know you well; that's clear,
no doubt . . .
so what the heck are you about?

If you weren't shy,
you'd know that
I couldn't embarrass you
more than you
embarrass yourself.

Rescue

Hi! I'm the expert of the "feel good" show.
Wrote the books that help you know.
I wow 'em on the stages
with my attitude courageous.
"Yes! I'm positive" yells the act
while my brain below is under attack.

My caved-in brain,
in primal pain
fighting hard to know my name.

My dearest friend,
you want to help.
You're throwing me your line,
hoping I won't suffocate,
that you'll get to me in time.

Your loving shines in sunlight open.
You receive what I grieve
and you're a-hopin'
that I don't die before I wake.
That I will make this prison break.

This struggle for my sanity is not a folly grave.
It's just more rocks keep tumbling,

burying me in waves.

So, please stand by; I know you're there.
It's just hard now to show I care.
If I return to sunshine,
clear and sane,
it's because you stayed to call my name.

Peace Talks

Tell the truce.

If the Shrew Fits, Swear it

Don't shut down,
just shut up.

"You know it's Dogwood by its bark."

Uncle Charley

Your sweet self touches me:
You have built your life upon
bricks of quiet caring for others.
I think of those babies
that you delivered on kitchen
tables and the time you took to understand
with love.

My love for you tumbles about
the smallest corner of your room.
My heart is open,
because you have touched me.

Be well.
Be joyous.
Be...
Charley.

Look Who Came To Town

Look who came to town
and turned us all upside-down.
Who took our time and social graces
and slapped us sorely across our faces.

Is she hope or is she scourge
as she pulls the covers off our words?
Angel or devil? Friend or foe?
She's scared us silly, that I know.

She blew the whistle on our games,
spoke of love and called us names.
We withstand snow and handle blizzard,
but, what to do with this strange wizard?

Don't neglect

when you connect

to expect respect.

Don't Eat With Your Mouth Full

Now that we've asked you to change
all those behaviors of yours:
just relax and be yourself.

The more you observe,
the more you observe.

If you see what I mean.

Do Whatever

Do whatever you need to do.
That's the love I give to you.
Burn off your energy,
let off your steam.
I'll stand by and watch
I'm on your team.

Say the words you have to say.
Connect with me or go away.
Do with me what you need to grow.
I accept where you put me, I want you to know.

I can only love you the way I do,
though it may not fit your need.
You can only love me the way you do,
it's the nature of our creed.

You feel misunderstood and so do I.
We can't be each other, even if we try.
For we are each unique; no two humans are the same,
and misunderstanding is life's cosmic game.

So go with your energy,
I'm standing by
with the sea and the soil
and a piece of the sky.

Tom

Tom, you are a gift.
Your crackle-sparkling words
ignite sparkle-crackling wonder
in me.

I'm glad that you,
in my presence,
have disrobed:
Dropping calcified deadness,
and standing naked
in your raw
and vulnerable beauty.

As you embrace the boy within you,
you stand enormous in your manhood.
Your words which freely flow
from you — they become you.

For me, Tom,
you are a gift.
A man of words:
A silent gentle man.

Threads unbroken if love is spoken.

C Section

My dearest friend I look to the
bottom of your purest of most blue eyes.
Waiting in the spotlights. Holding your calm hand.
My cauterized fear sticks silently to the white walls.

The doctor's suturing, picking and probing your
   gorgeous ripe belly.
Violating walls in search of buried treasure.
Dumbstruck time drip in rhythm to the I.V.
Then Linnea Britt: plumped and precious'
heralds with a cry.
And we weep, too, over the joy of her perfection-
touched by the immensity of her smallest cry.

I look into your blue eyes and see existence.
You a timeless woman.
You a warrior triumphant.

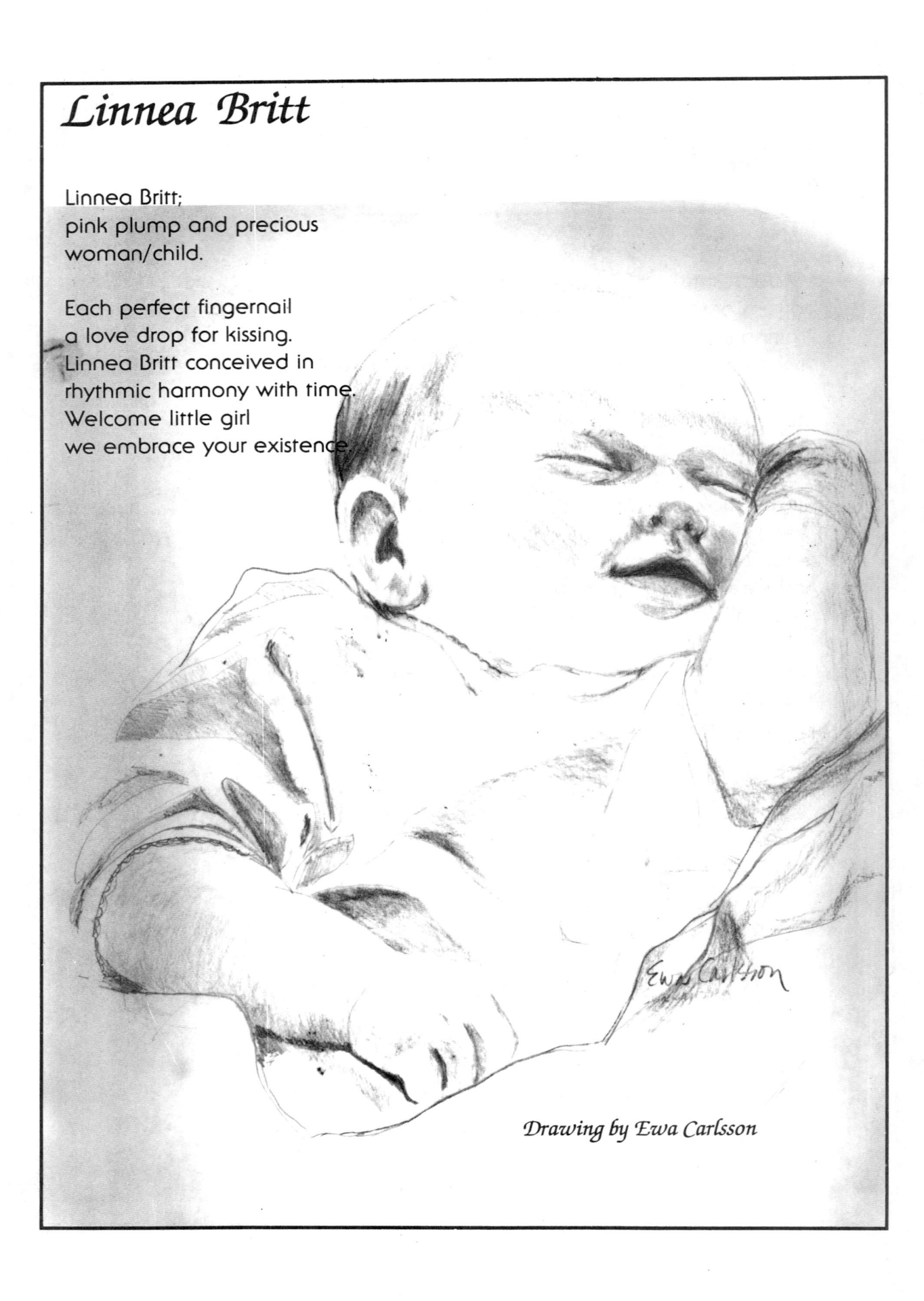

Linnea Britt

Linnea Britt;
pink plump and precious
woman/child.

Each perfect fingernail
a love drop for kissing.
Linnea Britt conceived in
rhythmic harmony with time.
Welcome little girl
we embrace your existence

Drawing by Ewa Carlsson

My grandpa

My grandpa was a tailor for the Czar
and his handmade coat smelled like
places from afar.

My grandpa was a square, tight package
with a round, shiny head and
eloquent fingers that he'd
wrap around a chair leg so he'd
lift the whole chair just like
an Olympic torch.

With those fingers
he'd strum my arm and he'd
sing rhythmic lullabies,
sweeter than Russian pastry,
vibrating me like a
concert piano.

On our walks,
I would watch those fingers
stitch mysteriously
into the pocket of his perfect coat
pulling out
semi-sweet chocolate squares,
one by one,
to put upon my tongue.

My grandpa's fingernails
were fairy tales.
After all,
my grandpa was a tailor for the Czar.

Fijians

Magnificent, solid brown beings;
open faces framed by black wholly halos.
Melding of the warm moist earth.
full-lipped smiles.
Diction slow, perfect.
Feet like puppies
and eyes:

Eyes chocolate kisses,
wrapping a star.

Man

Solid, sane, sensuous, silly,
submits in surrender,
assertive and clever.
His faces so many
in my inward eye;
playful, provocative,
hidden surprise.

Master or slave,
he does them both well,
asleep or awake,
the deepest of wells.

He fathoms forever,
my beautiful friend,
though it's just our beginning,
with him there's no end.

"Ma, look at those eyes!

They look like two ping pong balls with flies on them!

Battle With Time

I fought a battle with Time before we became acquainted,
   Time and I.
At first I ignored him. (Ignorance)
Then I noticed him keeping company with some old
   and battered folks I'd pass on the street.

Once I even stood by a young man as rejecting Time
   ran out on him,
     and I mourned his loss,
     and cried bitter hateful tears and knew that we,
       Time and I,
     could never be friends.

And then one day, or else a year,
Time stood silently at my mirror,
and while I watched, giddy Time began to dance upon my
   face, leaving laughing footprints all about my eyes.

I fought a battle with Time before we became acquainted.
Before, without an agency or reference
but just for old times sake
   . . . we became roommates.

De Part

Hair today,
Gone tomorrow.

Blurring Time

Blurring time;
smearing colors well-defined,
Fading in mist of memory,
I glimpse your smile,
the tenderness of your
warm hands.

Fogging in and out;
your name echoes through distant halls
as I recall fragments of our sacred past.

My fuzzy mind forgets
what my heart remembers.

Ooh, Those Hands!

Ooh, those hands:
sliding oil slicks,
moving little valleys of muscles and nerves.
Exploring bone continents.

Doors locked tight in stagnant tension,
and despair,
flung open;
in the light of those hands.

Energized and tame,
I breathe gently to your name
and hands.

Flesh upon flesh,
you have borned me
afresh.

English Showers

God tears fall
and thus it grows,
the bloomin' flower,
the bloody rose.

RELIGION & DRUGS

A MAIZE SING

God

Elusive God,
hidden behind concrete images
and concepts
and religion
and words.
Peek-a-boo God
touches your nervous system
when you stick your finger
into the light socket
of ultimate mystery
and feel, fleeting,
that profound mystery

that profound mystery of your
very
own
existence.

You radiate God when you,
without a face,
touch timeless space.
Eternity hides in what we call time
and beyond the words dwells
the sublime.

Beauty beside me,
beauty behind me,
beauty in front of me,
beauty to the right of me,
beauty to the left of me,
beauty above me,
beauty below me.

From dust to dust,
womb to tomb.

We are the fiber;
God is the loom.

Close To Thee

For me,
some places are closer to God.
The cliffs (bold and craggy)
along the Big Sur.
Yosemite
(laced lucious with waterfalls)
The quiet redwood trees:
(pillars holding up the sky)
Haleakala Crater
(with its moon walks and rainbows)
Santa Fe
(adobe rich with Indians)
spiced by chili pepper sunsets.
Ireland
(rock walls and haystacks).
A mountain
(fresh powdered in snow).
Misty morning in a forest.
A gurgle brook.
A kitten yielding neutral in my lap.
A herd of elephants at a watering hole.

Caves, mountains, oceans, waterfalls and streams:
All sofas where God comes to sit
(naked and ready to chat)
and whispers silent to the night,
and sings joyously in the morning light.

It's only when I go inside,
   buried and defended in my head,
   that I think,
   perhaps, that God is dead.

Enlightenment
Replace why with wise.

Repeating A Mantra
Living at ohm,
taking up resonance.
In-chanting.
A trance former.

Ms. Tickle
A miss under stood.

Free
No charge.

The Religion

"We are right," they shout
while the silent "you are wrong"
is the flip side of their song.

In their clusters large or small,
it makes them feel so tall.
So they shout out with their might,
"We are right! We are right!"

By pitying the others,
they betray them as their brothers.
Building walls up as they "spread the word."
Perhaps, God should be seen, not heard.

Who Doesn't Love A Flower

Is there one who doesn't love a flower?
Or has not swallowed extra breath when
surprised by a rainbow?
Is there one who hasn't smiled at a
nubile babe or ducklings wiggled tail?

Is there one too soured to enjoy
a concert of fresh air at morning.
A taste bud which doesn't chortle when
meeting a fresh fruit?

Is there one who's heart is locked
from brothers and sisters of this Earth
and finds no purpose in their birth?

That one resides in each of us:
made of pain and forgotten trust.

I am my own child
deserving my love;
a perfect soul; a godly nub.
When I give myself time, compassion
and love,
I learn to grow and come to know
that I am perfect (that is me)
and beauty floods the world I see.

Is there one who doesn't love a flower?
No, only one pained and forgotten.

Reality is for people who can't tolerate drugs.

Love Drunk

I'm drunk on rung-up-love-you-booze,
hung-up, fuzzy-brain-spread-the-news.
Forgotten schedules, out of gas,
freeway exits I shouldn't have passed.

Out of time, into space,
a world overlaid upon your face
Dreaming or waking, I can't tell,
I'm stoned by your voice, your touch, your smell.

I go through withdrawals when we're apart,
give me a fix of your clear-me-brain-heart.

Obsession

Was there life before you?
I can't remember;
my thoughts are too crowded with your name.

Did ever I think other thoughts
before your every detail filled the tiniest
crevice of my mind?

Your shadows blanket me asleep or awake.
You are my zen meditation;
I contemplate each facet of you into infinity.

Lost I am to the warmth of your eyes and my
hunger for your body.

Was there life before you?
I can't remember.

No Con Test

No mister he;
my liqui date
with tranquil ize
is inti mate me.

Recurrent Training
hermetically sealed in bull

Flap and flurry scribbles,
dramatic long-wind drivel,
monosyllabic garble. Verbose tome;
dull, lulling drone.

Pablumed repetition.
Annual certification.
Government regulation.
Mandatory education.

Simple concepts:
Complicated.
My lovely brain:
Contaminated.

Hell Loose Sin O Gin

Drink it up,
throw it down.
Party time;
paint the town

Bottoms up.
Ease your pain.
One little toddy—
No social strain.

And I witness your suicide,
insidiously away you slide,
pickled in your social brew
killing you slowly

(what can I do?)

So pardon me if I seem unkind,
but alcohol has pickled your mind.

Oh Brother

My brother Marc told me he was a drug dealer:
ate prophylactics filled with substance abuse
to bring the stuff in.

He made those runs
with other parents' nicest sons,
(subsidized his monthly allotment)
became a lawyer and a doctor.

He sued
me and our older brother
so he could pocket more money
from the estate of our mother.

My brother is handsome,
like Omar Sharif,
and says he's out to bury me.
When he was small,
I was his second mom
and he said he wanted to marry me.

My brother, Marc,
is reputable.
(Uses LSD occasional)
Beat up his fiance,
(only once)
and has good manners
at the table.

My brother, Marc,
in his doctor's smocks,
is admired and respected.
He writes prescriptions,
pays his bills,
and is societally protected.

Seasons change us in our lives
(It's amazing what we discover)
that little boy I once adored;
he's heavy, he's my brother.

Sprinkled Spaghetti
Happy New You

Slosh the bubbly
Auld Lang Syne.
Start afresh
with passing time.

Toast and boast
my cup of tea,
slightly pickled in the glee.

Folks dressed up in
lace and glitter.
Music, hors d' ouvres
hostess aflitter.

Some cling to walls
and history,
depressed beyond the revelry.
Others,
   once again,
for the very first time,
resolve a diet or making a dime.

We toot our horns
with paper tongue,
giddy and shouting,
having fun.

Twangled tongue,
screamers and spaghetti.
Sloshed to the gills . . .
A toast? I'm ready!

Happy New You,
Happy New Me,
out with the old;
te, he, he.

We ended this year
with folly engaging.
Next year will
bring a hangover raging.

Half Two

If you have to,
don't have two,
half two!

Shock Therapy

Boo! Be. Trapped.

Your body is a holy owned subsidiary of your soul.

DEATH

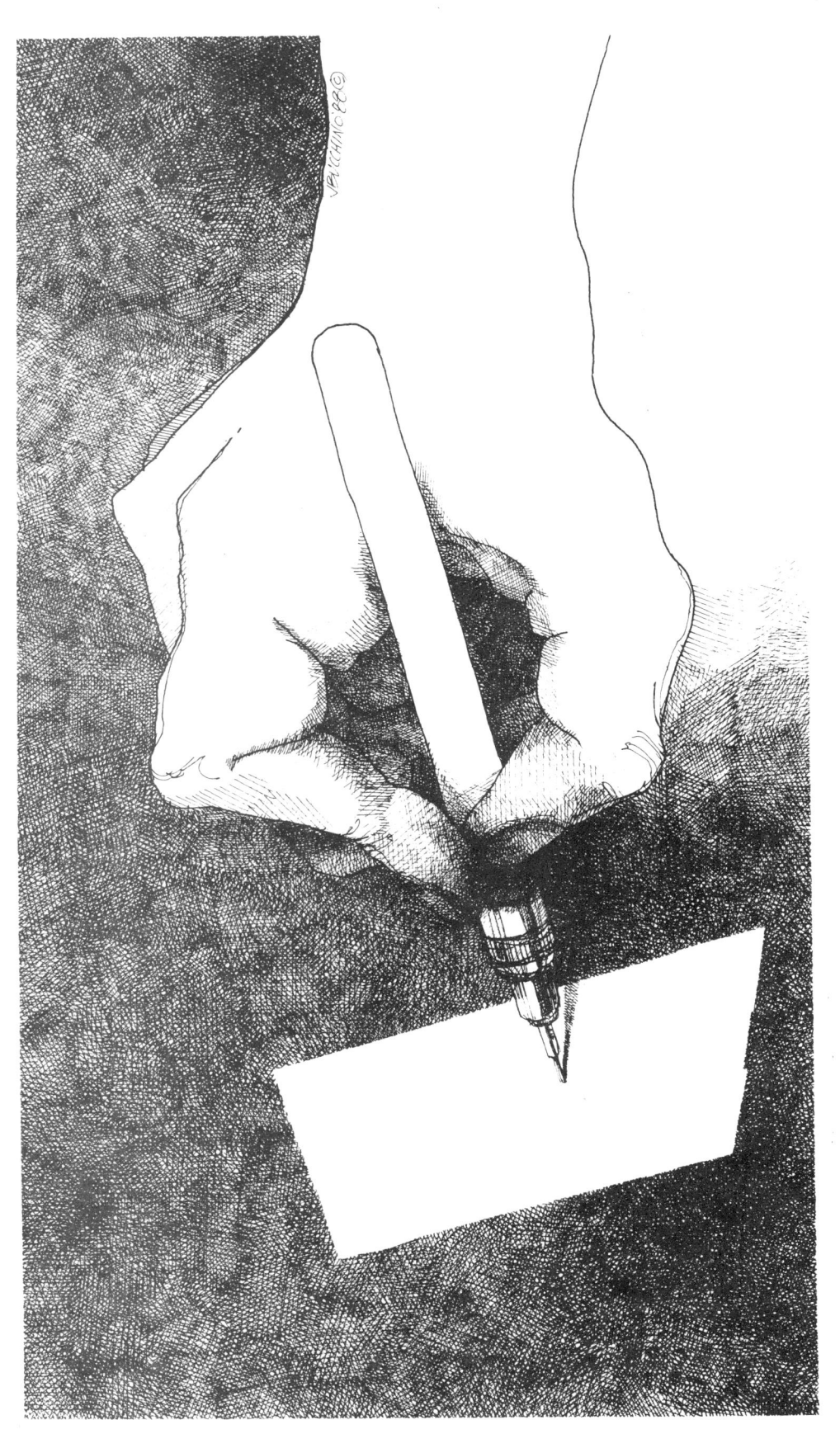

DRAWING A BLANK

It's O.K. to kill time;

time is going to kill you.

Tutankhamen

Even Tutankhamen
(hermetically sealed in pyramid power
dressed in gold
wrapping and trappings;
packed like a bullet train
with wives and servants
furniture and toys)
died alone.

All the gaping eyes of
tourists, cameras, robbers
and museum keepers
don't offer company.
(to his dismay)
Nothing consecrated his decay.
He went away
Alone that day.

The tides of women's groins
pumping life forth as so many
grains until each in their
turn ends as Tut.
We are all shifting sand.
Visitors only for our space;
shifting sand
without a face.

Funeral Home

This room
(tastefully appointed)
holds us tightly
in a still fist.

In wild array
(the baskets and sprays).
Michelle rests her hand on her belly
(fatting with child).
Odessa weeps silent in her grieving.

Couched in textured beige;
(Dressed in Sunday best)
Paul is here at rest.

Embalmed and bloated
(in satin and polished mahogany);
his mouth a sneaky silent smile,

proud that he went out in style.

Photo by Shelley Stockwell

It's Great To Be Alive

Max was the life of the party.

"I go for the beer, not the foam," he would say. And he'd twist his stogie one-eighth turn with his tongue, pat his little basketball tummy, and chuckle.

"Shut up and deal," Harry would bellow. The poker chips and pretzels would quiver.

Some things are destiny. For thirty-five years the guys gathered in Max and Ethel's basement behind the heavy door labeled "Max's room, enter at your own risk." And the five of them would join in the holy communion of beer, cards and nudie pin-ups. Any Friday there they'd be. There wasn't a woman or snowstorm to keep them apart. Max, Harry, Bump, Gator, and Bobby Baynes. Bad jokes, bad breath, arguing like wildcats; they were tight.

Thus it was that there was a shocked and hollow silence that filled their minds this particular Friday night. Max had died two days earlier. Max Barclay . . .

"Got up in the morning and died on the john," announced Ethel between wails and sobs. "He didn't even eat his breakfast."

The news of Max's demise spread like high speed ether. There must have been fifty people sitting in the Barclays' tiny, warm living room. The ladies clucked their tongues in rhythm to the clattering of cups and saucers.

"Max would have liked such a large turnout at his wake," Ethel was saying proudly.

Gator sat in one corner picking uncomfortably at a piece of invisible lint.

"Why would Max go and do a thing like this to us?" he mumbled.

"I miss the little fart already," said Harry, bobbing his balding head rhythmically.

"I understand they've got his coffin downstairs in the card room," said Bump. "Somehow I'd feel better down there. Care to join me?"

He got up and headed for the basement, the three others following closely behind. The room smelled heavily of embalming fluid. Bobby Baynes headed directly to the refrigerator, took out a six pack of Rolling Rock and put it on the table. The rest of the guys stood stone still, looking into the carved wooden casket.

"He's a cute little fellow, that Max," said Gator and one lone tear dripped off the end of his nose.

"You cryin' Gator?" bellowed Harry. "Hell, you guys look like this is the end of the world. Now, what would Max think if he saw us all blubbering like a bunch of broads? Pussies, he'd say. A bunch of pink pussies! Dammit, Max, we ain't gonna send you off with a silly tea party. We're gonna toast your little waxy face and wish you a great journey. Whata ya say guys?"

"Here, here!" they cheered.

"Here's to Max!" and they each threw down a beer. And another. And another.

Later they began punctuating the beer with Early Times. Bump turned the radio on full bore. They drifted into a familiar patter of football and getting laid, the ashtray swelling into a smoking grey volcano, laughter and philosophy mixing with the smoke, belches, booze, blaring music and embalming fluid.

Finally, the music lifted Bobby Baynes from his chair, and he started dancing an Irish Jig. Harry joined him and they stumbled and laughed and held each other up. Gator joined in.

"Care to dance my dear?" asked Gator, extending his calloused hand toward Bump.

"I'll sit this one out, thank you," replied Bump, popping another beer.

"If Max was here he'd sure as hell have accepted my invitation. Why Max was a regular twinkle toes," mused Gator.

"Max is here, you ass," belched Harry and in his exuberance lost his balance and made a three-point landing across the coffin.

Laughter filled the smoke.

"Hey, Max, would you like to dance?" asked Harry. And he reached into the wooden box and lifted Max to a rigid upright position, holding him in a bear hug. Max's dead weight didn't hinder Harry a bit.

"Come on, Max, admit it, ain't it great to be alive?" and he spun and bobbed to the raucous music, Max's little black church shoes dragging along.

For an instant the others stood staring in disbelief. And then the intoxication of Harry's words and the music filled the moment.

"It's great to be alive," was the most profound thing ever heard. The words reverberated in their heads.

"It's great to be alive!" they shouted. Bump jammed a stogie between Max's clenched teeth and his inside cheek.

"It's great to be alive," and the nudie pin-ups and gray bricks blurred past. They whirled and danced and spun.

Ethel heard noises in the basement. She hesitated before the heavy door. "Max's room, enter at your own risk" it said.

Accident (The Coast's Not Clear)

If it wasn't for the safety glass
strewn like crystal confetti,
or the car split open like a soup can,
or the polka dots of blood jumping out
like chicken pox,
or the coroner waiting for the police pictures,
or the Colorado Highway Patrol,
in hats dangling flaccid gold tassles,
or one ski boot, then
a tennis shoe
and some loose change,
or that one young man,
deader than dying,
stunned white and bloody
on Christmas day.

If it wasn't for that:

I would have enjoyed stopping here
to look at the view.

Let's not come this way again.

The Rooster

Rebecca Wilson wasn't invited to be born, a fact her alcoholic mother slurred out regularly, sandwiched among her sloshing centrifugal thoughts. "I was almost famous and your father came along. Damn baseball players. He got me good...if I hadn't been knocked up...oh, here, kitty, kitty...care for a crumpet? Ha, ha...a line from Hamlet, or was it omelet?

Invited or not, Rebecca was here. She had great energy and mental power. Her humor was subtle and sparkling and her grades were straight 'A's. She had inherited her mother's striking red hair and glistening green eyes. She seemed to be climbing toward her father's tremendous height (he was 6'6" tall) and a small elephant's weight. She was, by far, the brightest and largest girl in her 3rd grade class.

"It is a pleasure to have Rebecca in my class. Her citizenship is much above average. She is very polite and soft spoken," Miss Pringle had written in the comment section of her report card.

Everyone shared Miss Pringle's belief. Rebecca was easy, well mannered and non-threatening.

"My daughter's just like me," her dad would croon as he petted her red locks, "good and quiet. Quietly good."

The rooster had a different opinion. The rooster had known Rebecca for two years. For two years she had punctuated 3:30 p.m. for him more dramatically than he punctuated 6:00 a.m. for the world. Five days a week he'd see her coming across the field; her huge, round form slouching over armloads of books. She would walk directly to the wire walls that surrounded him, put her books on the ground and begin.

"Hi, Stupid," she said, picking up a stick. "How do you like that," and she'd stab the stick through the fencing. "Stupid, stupid, stupid," she chanted.

He flapped wildly, avoiding the poking stick. She charged the cage again, chiding and cajoling. The rooster would go mad, flapping; blood in his pin-pointy eyes, kill in his jumping, slicing talons, and screeching his death scream, he'd lunge at the huge round animal, aiming his sharp claws at her flowing, stringy comb. All his power and strength in that war charge and the cruel, cutting wires jamming him to an abrupt, smashing halt. Stunned, he'd fall to the soil, his green-black feathers gummed with blood, earth and rooster droppings.

Rebecca would laugh her cruelest laugh and begin again. "I hate you, I hate you, I hate you," she'd scream, throwing rocks, spitting and hissing.

Again and again the rooster would jump and claw and attack. Again and again the forgotten fence would repel him. Finally, Rebecca would pick up her books and continue her walk home.

It is difficult to know exactly how capable your basic rooster is of deep or clearly defined thoughts. Yet, it appeared that after the years of reenacting this same scene, the rooster's mood toward Rebecca had shifted. Tension had yielded to anger; anger to fury, and now to a single-minded vengence that even the smallest of brains can intensify.

It was a damp and foggy January day. Farmer Benson had a terrible cold. Benny, the farmer's 11-year-old son, had to do the chores. Disgruntled, he fed the horse, milked the cows, collected the eggs from the hens and rushed across the field to the small coop to scatter corn for the rooster. If he didn't hurry, he'd miss baseball practice.

Rebecca was in fine spirits this particular day. She had just won the all-school spelling bee, her father was home for his annual break before spring training, and her mother was calm and sober.

Rebecca came skipping and singing across the muddy field, her yellow galoshes splashing puddles. So ebullient was she that she almost passed the rooster without so much as one thrown rock. But the "rooster ritual," by now, was rote. So, out of habit, she grabbed a handful of rocks and walked toward the coop.

"Hi, Dummy," she said as she approached. The rooster backed off to the far side of the fencing, his feathers puffing, preparing for war. Rebecca heaved the largest stone in her hand. "How do you like that?". . .and the rooster attacked. He charged slightly off to the right of the large girl. He ran headlong into the small gated portion of the coop. The gate had been left unlatched! It flung open with the impact of the crazed bird. Kill glazed his little eyes as he jumped clawing and flying toward the enemy, missing her by inches.

Rebecca shrieked in horror. Vomit filled her mouth. She threw her books and rocks in the air and started to run, her fat thighs colliding with each step, perspiration steaming the inside of her yellow plastic rain coat. Running was not Rebecca's forte, but she was doing a splendid job of staying in front of the rooster. She must have been five yards in the lead when her plastic shoes stuck fast in the gummy, slick mud. She fell face first, her palms stinging with abrasion, mud in her teeth and eyes. The rooster was flapping toward her, crowing a warwhoop, announcing his assured victory. Rebecca wallowed like a hippo through the sludge, scraping her knee. Finally, she clambered to her feet, her galoshes left standing in the mud like two small yellow tombstones.

The rooster was lethally close. He was only inches from shredding her to bits when Rebecca reached her back porch, opening the screen door and slamming it behind. The rooster sliced at the door, the screen stunning him like chicken cooping.

The great commotion of Rebecca's hysterical screaming and the squalling and bashing of the rooster brought Mr. Wilson to his feet. He was a good man, he did what had to be done. If a dog goes rabid, you put it to sleep. If a crazed fighting cock is on the loose . . . He grabbed a shovel in his powerful hand and marched outside.

Rebecca ran to her room and hid under the bed. She heard the screaming screech of the rooster, and repeated sound of metal against earth. Then there was silence.

Drawing by Paula Suarez

Heart Attack

Trials and fibrillations.

The Helping Hand

"Glenda Dudd's family name gave her a birthright of dullsville," my friend would say. That was a matter beyond dispute, so I just let the subject slide by with the Nat King Cole record and copious amounts of Coca Cola. At age 16, I had a mission. I was a helper to the less fortunate. A pubescent Robin Hood taking my time and energy from the nubile popular and giving freely to the fat, acne-ridden high school rejects. "Stray dogs," I called them, and I ran the kennel.

Thus it was that Glenda Dudd came to my attention. Physically she was rather a mediocre loser. Other than an extra 70 pounds or so, she had a nondescript browness about her. She was so physically lackluster that it was possible that she could totally evaporate from cognitive space and time, were it not for one pronounced characteristic: she talked incessantly. Not about things of consequence, like boys or clothes or who's dating whom, but rather things like, well, it was difficult to say - it all came out sounding like a 747 engine.

"Oh look at that tree," she would begin. "It reminds me of my Uncle Raymond. Uncle Raymond lives in Ventura. He's married to Aunt Sylvia. They have 6 kids: Little Dougie, Constance, Paul, Becky, Bobby Lynn and well, let's see, oh yes, the baby, Cary. Uncle Raymond has two cousins that live in Oxnard. One's name is Oliver . . ." and off she would go into the wild blue yonder.

Glenda seemed to enjoy her "chats" with me so much that she took to calling me up every afternoon after school. I found I could answer the phone, ask a simple question like, "How are you?" and then put the handset on the dresser and clean my room for the next 20 minutes, pausing once or twice to utter an "uh huh" into the mouthpiece.

We might have gone on indefinitely in this pattern had not an extraordinary occurrence happened to Glenda. She was asked out on a date — the first time in her life! She called me breathlessly. "He asked me out, he asked me out" she squealed. "This weekend, to dinner and a movie! Oh my God, oh my dear, sweet God!"

The "he" was George Salmon, class of '61 and famous for using the same handkerchief for blowing his nose and cleaning his eyeglasses, playing with himself, and sporting half a tooth in the front. George was as lean as Glenda was stout. But, such is life, he'd asked her out.

"Glenda, I'll be over first thing Saturday morning and help you get ready. Would you like that?"

"Oh yes, thank you. Thank you. That reminds me of San Clemente. I went there last year on a Saturday, I think it was the 16th of March. They have a street there called Elm Street. It has lots of little white houses. The first house by the stop sign has a red mailbox . . ."

I arrived at Glenda's house very early that Saturday morning. After all, I needed all the time I could get. That gave me from morning 'til 7 pm to educate her as to the fine points of successful dating. I curled her hair, polished her nails, applied copious amounts of mascara, rouge and Tangee lipstick. I had Glenda model each outfit of her vast brown and beige collection of tents until we found the "perfect" one. All this activity was punctuated with teenage etiquette tips which I conferred upon her. "Always let the man open doors for you, even if it seems to take forever. Sit quietly in the car until he comes around and opens the door. Men like to know you expect to be treated like a lady."

"To kiss goodnight on the first date or not to kiss goodnight, that is the question." Glenda rambled and expounded her conflicts over this moral dilemma as I plucked each misgrown eyebrow.

"Glenda, I want you to listen for a minute. If you hear nothing else, hear this: Men are very egotistical," I said, "they love to talk about themselves. It's your duty as a woman to be a good listener and ask the right questions so you can get a guy to talk about himself. That's by far the most important thing to remember. Don't say too much, just ask a few questions. Keep him talking about himself, he'll love you for it."

I had finessed her to shut up. I was a perfect diplomat. I knew how to fix up people like Glenda. She'd knock him dead. The romance of the century unfolds!

Throughout the day I drove my central thesis home. She even seemed to have listened. And so, I left her house. I felt heady, like a victorious coach; my team was trained, prepared and ready for action. It will be another doomed life set straight; such a sweet reward for my "save a soul" crusade. She and the guy with the smudged eyeglasses riding smilingly off into the sunset, prompting visions of a family of little Salmon and a white house with a red mailbox.

I was awakened at 7 am the next morning by the demanding ring of the phone by my bed. "Hello," I mumbled.

"Oh, Dolly, it was marvelous, just like a movie. He had this neat car, a blue '57 Ford with gray interior and tuck and roll. The car had an am/fm radio, air conditioning, and automatic transmission. We went to Pucchios restaurant. It's the one on Pacific Avenue, 2942 Pacific, I believe. The one next to Al's Shoe Repair. I ate 7 breadsticks and butter. The antipasto had 5 slices of salami, 2 artichoke hearts and 5 little funny rubbery things that were delicious. There were 14 tables, I counted them. At the table by the front window was a man wearing a white shirt and bow tie. He was with a lady with gray hair and 3 kids. The first one, a boy, was about 14 years old and was wearing . . ." The droning lullaby of words drifted me out into a lovely sleep. I was awakened by an intonation change coming from the handset on my pillow.

"Dolly, are you listening?"

"Oh, yeah, sure."

"Then why didn't you answer my question?"

"I guess my mind wandered. Please repeat it."

"Guess what George was wearing?" Ebulliently she continued — on and on. She had a great time, I concluded. It must have been one hell of a date.

"Glenda, Glenda, Glenda, one thing and I must go. Did he kiss you good night?"

"No, but he parked right in front of Mrs. Richardson's camelia bush. You know Mrs. Richardson has 12 different varieties of camelias. She has the light pink Debutante ones, those semi-double flame ones with the big yellow stamins, and..."

George never asked Glenda out again. One day, at a student council meeting, I pulled George's beautiful, younger sister aside. "Renee, how come George never asked Glenda out again?"

"You know," she replied. "It was the craziest thing. George was so excited about taking her out. That's all he talked about. But after that date he said she was too quiet for him."

"Oh," I gasped behind a painted smile. I was flooding with the crushing, hard core reality. Dolly Do-good's traveling salvation show was running out of steam.

Two days later, I closed the kennel, but the scars of my guilt run deep. Glenda 21 years later, I've heard is still 70 pounds overweight. She teaches high school history and bible class at her church. She's never had another date. As for George; well I'd rather not know.

"Did I frighten you too much?"

"No, you frightened me just enough."

Photo by Bryce Stockwell

You can't worry about life forever.

If you start at the end you're finished.

Prism Girl

(By Betsy Mewborn Moreland)

We were four, you came knocking at my door.
You were small, and I wasn't very tall.
You smiled at me and I could see
right then you would be my friend.

We were five, we were so glad to be alive.
And your sun, it would shine on everyone.
Prism girl, rainbow swirling hair,
And I knew you'd care.

Innocence and trusting were the names we bore.
It wasn't until later we learned what tears were for . . .

We were fifteen, you became a beauty queen.
I was bright, it was my only guiding light,
Or so I thought, and so I fought my fears
For so many years.

Now, here we are. Yes, we have come so very far,
Or have we just relearned the way it feels to trust
Like a child growing wild and free.
You are you and I am me.
You and I are still we.

Shelley Lessin Stockwell is an artist of life who believes that to live rich and lusty you must listen to your inner wisdom, respect your body with healthy food and air, tell the truth, go for your dreams, and love yourself.

Shelley lives in a white house with red trim overlooking the Pacific Ocean. She enjoys herself, her family, and her friends. She is a professional hypnotherapist who simultaneously has worked as a TWA flight attendant for the past 20 years. Her travels have given her a chance to meet Masai warriors in Kenya, headhunters on the Amazon in Peru and royalty from Tonga. She has made deep friendships with people all over the world!

Shelley is a popular motivational speaker and an award-winning member of Toastmasters and The National Speakers Association. She is the star of Dimension Cable's **The Shelley Show**; where she showcases her abundant humor, poetry and love of life.

She holds an honorary Doctor of Divinity degree and conducts beautiful humanistic wedding ceremonies. Her news paper columns and short stories have earned her many awards. Drop her a note and tell her what's on your mind: she would adore hearing from you.

Write to Shelley c/o CREATIVITY UNLIMITED PRESS 30819 Casilina, Rancho Palos Verdes, Ca. 90274

BOOKS

CREATIVITY UNLIMITED PRESS
Is proud to offer the following items
for you and your loved ones:

INSIDES OUT
by **Shelley Lessin Stockwell**

$6.95

Plain talk poetry guaranteed to speak to you where you really live. If you want to awaken your vitality and truly enjoy yourself, this is your book!

"....Sprinkled throughout are short thoughts and quippy asides - amusing and anecdotal"
— Focus on Books

"A beautiful, heart touching book. I urge you all to read it."
— Toni Grant, KABC Talk Radio

"There is a lot of humor in this book, but you can learn a lot too. There is wisdom along with the humor . . . it's really a fantastic book."
— Madelyn Camrud, WDAZ ABC-TV

"Shows how poetry can help see inside yourself. Maybe you'll like what you see."
— Bill Smith, Channel 11 News

132 Pages / Perfect Bound
ISBN #0-12559-00-4
LCN #83-710-30

GREAT RELATIONS:
Do-It-Yourself Counseling For Couples

by **Dr. Alex Lessin**

$9.95

Practical, easy-to-do steps for you and your beloved to grow as individuals and create more joy, zest & impact. All this in 6 easy lessons. A must for couples!

"A delightfully practical guide for the journey through the mountains and valleys of living in a relationship."

Alan Cohen, Author of:
The Dragon Doesn't Live Here Anymore

Whenever I perform a wedding I give the bride & groom my heartfelt blessings and a copy of Dr. Alex Lessin's book Great Relations."
— Alicia Bay Laurel, Weddings Made In Maui

ISBN #0-945596-00-6

SELF HYPNOSIS:
Smiles On Your Face, Money In Your Pocket

by **Shelley Lessin Stockwell**

$9.95

SOON TO BE RELEASED!

How to use it as a powerful tool for yourself, your family and your friends. Teaches you what hypnosis is & uses the untapped power of your mind to make your dreams become a reality.

Learn:
- ★ The 30 Second Zap
- ★ 42 Personal Affirmations
- ★ Hypnosis Script
- ★ Dream Charting
- ★ How to Vanish "Loser" Attitudes & Replace Them With Successful Ones
- ★ How To Be A Money Magnet

ISBN #0-912559-17-9

SEX & OTHER TOUCHY SUBJECTS

(THE BOOK)

by **Shelley Lessin Stockwell**

BOOK INCLUDES **FREE** "BOOK ON CASSETTE" OFFER!

$14.95

This "Gift Of The Year" award winning book tackles love, money, sex, drugs, religion, Mom, Dad, apple pie and death. Hilariously funny; profoundly sensitive.

"Shelley has an eerie talent for writing MY very thoughts...To enjoy this book is to truly enjoy myself."
— Kris Blake, Magic Mirrors

340 Pages
ISBN #0-912559-12-8
LCN #88-71940

SEX & OTHER TOUCHY SUBJECTS

(THE CASSETTE TAPE)

A most unusual book on tape from the best seller of the same title.

Shelley Lessin Stockwell's songs and words are guaranteed to make you roar, sing, and celebrate the rites of Spring. This tape features the popular singles: **Static Grit On My CB** and **The Dating Game Reject**. Also: **Yes, I'm Positive** and **Frustration is the 'F' Word**.

The songs are brilliantly arranged by **Frank Unzuata** and performed by **Shelley, Frank,** and **Betsy Moreland**.

60 Minutes
$10.00 Value
ISBN #0-912559-13-6

AUDIO CASSETTES

THE MONEY TAPE

$10.00

Created by **Dr. Joan Lessin** and **Ed Seykota,** World famous commodities trader

Includes the workbook **The Way To Abundance"** by Dr. Alex Lessin.

"The Money Tape was the beginning of true prosperity in my life. It helped me feel good, not only about money, but about myself and my life. I love the combination of hypnosis, 'The Money Show', and the catchy tunes."

— Susan Bredesen, CEO, Public Relations Firm

"I got rid of a lot of subconscious beliefs that kept money from me, & opportunities for making money began to show up and haven't stopped.

— Robin Johnson, Music Promoter

"The Money Tape got me clear on my priorities and goals. It helped me see that I could create that green energy flow in many different ways.

— Barbara Purinton, Therapist

DEEP INTO A CALMING OCEAN

$10.00

by **Allen Kaufman**

Music proven to induce Alpha State.

"Seconds after starting your music cassette I found myself calm and relaxed . . . Thank you!"

— Bruce Rische

SELF HYPNOSIS AUDIO CASSETTES

closed eye meditations by Shelley Lessin Stockwell   Only $10.00 each

Lose Weight!
Lose unwanted pounds forever and gain energy and confidence.

Yes, You Can Quit Smoking
Save money, Breathe again and feel healthy.

No More Alcohol
Break free of alcohol. Feel your life again.

Peace and Calm
The perfect stress reducer. You need no tranquilizers.

Yes, I Can!
Achieve your personal goals and potentials.

No More Sugar Junkie
No more sugar blues. Feel alive; terrific!

Sleep, Beautiful Sleep
Sleep soundly and feel rested, at home or away. Good stress reduction.

Flight Attendant Well-Being
A perfect attitude adjuster. Face passengers feeling positive, happy.

Shelley Stockwell's self-hypnosis cassettes teach you to shed antiquated negative habits and replace them with the good habits you want for yourself.

Here is a sampling of the hundreds of letters we have on file:

"Thank you Shelley for giving me - ME!   — C.M., Grand Forks, North Dakota

"Your tapes have been a real blessing in my life"
                                              — D.R., San Francisco, CA

"FANTASTIC! You wonderful, crazy, creative woman. Thanks for sharing so much with everyone."   — V.R., Los Angeles, CA

Self Hypnosis Cassette Tapes
60 Minutes Each

OTHER AUDIO CASSETTES

U R WHAT U EAT & THE DINOSAUR RAP

$10.00

Created by
Shelley Lessin Stockwell, Hypnotherapist
Kathy Felker, Registered Dietitian & famous puppeteer,
Betsy Moreland, Special Education Teacher,
Frank Unzuata, "The Magic Music Man"
Spike, your basic dinosaur

"U R What U Eat teaches children an important nutritional message, while providing catchy refrains.   Reggae inspired embellishments make pleasant listening for adults as well and weightwatchers could use this for positive auto-suggestion." — Focus on Books

"The perfect antidote to junk food" — Judy Pastel, Mother

22 Minutes
ISBN #0-912559-14-4

MOMMY BUNNY'S GOING TO WORK

$10.00

by **Shelley Lessin Stockwell**

"A simple, reassuring song and story that can help parents enormously in dealing with their children's abandonment anxiety." — Ellen Hokanson, Focus on Books

"Before MOMMY BUNNY, Ryan threw a fit when I went to work. Now, he's happy and I don't feel guilty!" — Gayle Tritz, Flight Attendant

"Mommy rabbit left. Baby rabbit is happy and says I love you Mommy." — Suzy Brown, Age 4

ISBN #0-912559-16-0
ISBN #0-912559-06-3
(Flight Attendant Version)

COMPLIMENTARY CASSETTE COUPON

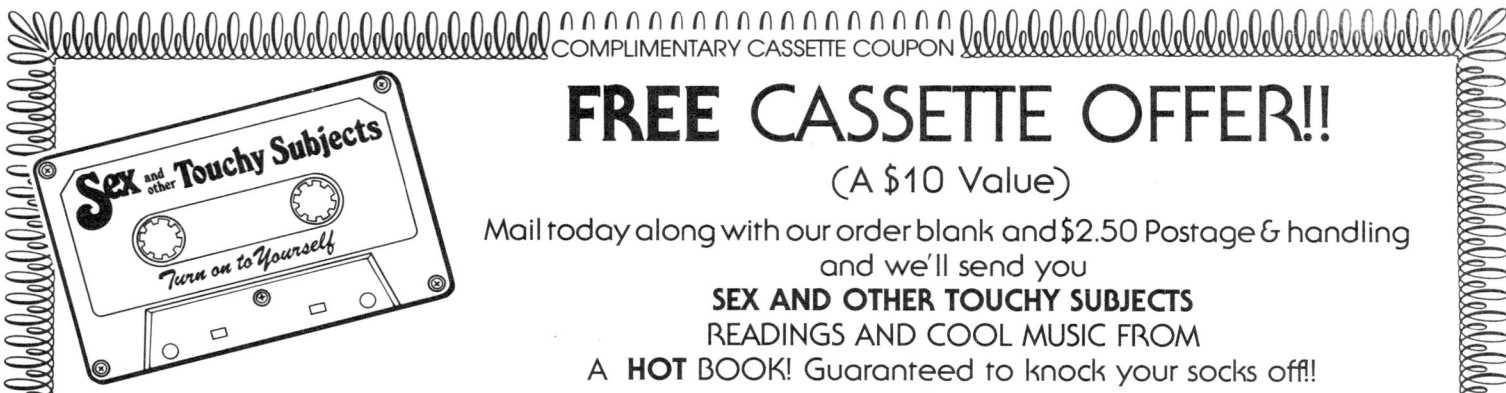

FREE CASSETTE OFFER!!
(A $10 Value)

Mail today along with our order blank and $2.50 Postage & handling and we'll send you
SEX AND OTHER TOUCHY SUBJECTS
READINGS AND COOL MUSIC FROM
A **HOT** BOOK! Guaranteed to knock your socks off!!

☐ **YES!** Please send me my FREE Cassette, **SEX & OTHER TOUCHY SUBJECTS!**

ORDERING INFORMATION
Please check the boxes of your choice (if more than one, please insert quantity)
Also available from Creativity Unlimited:

★ **BOOKS**
- ☐ INSIDES OUT .... $ 6.95
- ☐ GREAT RELATIONS 9.95
- ☐ HYPNOSIS (Smile On Your Face & $ In Your Pocket) 9.95
- ☐ SEX & OTHER TOUCHY SUBJECTS 14.95

★ **SELF HYPNOSIS CASSETTES**
- ☐ NO MORE SUGAR JUNKIE $10
- ☐ YES, I CAN QUIT SMOKING $10
- ☐ FLIGHT ATTENDANT WELL-BEING $10
- ☐ SLEEP, BEAUTIFUL SLEEP $10
- ☐ PEACE AND CALM $10
- ☐ YES! I CAN $10
- ☐ LOSE WEIGHT $10
- ☐ THE MONEY TAPE $10

★ **KIDS**
- ☐ MOMMY BUNNY'S GOING TO WORK $10
- ☐ U R WHAT U EAT $10

★ **MUSIC AND SONG**
- ☐ DEEP INTO A CALMING OCEAN $10
- ☐ SEX & OTHER TOUCHY SUBJECTS $10

SUBTOTAL
(California residents add 7¢ per dollar sales tax)
Foreign Countries please add $1.00 to the price of each publication.

PLUS $2.50 POSTAGE AND HANDLING PER ITEM

TOTAL

ALLOW 4-6 WEEKS FOR DELIVERY

FOR FAST ORDERING: CALL (213) 541-4844
Payment Method

☐ Check/Money Order
☐ Charge   ☐ VISA   ☐ MasterCard

Card No. _____

Expiration Date _____

_____
Card Holder's Signature

Please complete this page and mail to:

CREATIVITY UNLIMITED PRESS
30819 Casilina, Rancho Palos Verdes, CA 90274

PLEASE PRINT

NAME _____
ADDRESS _____
CITY _____ STATE _____
ZIP _____ PHONE ( ) _____

Give A Friend The Gift Of Love & Laughter!

Make someone happy!
Send them a book or tape today!
Give us their name, address and any greeting you wish
to send and we will mail it to them from you!

To order additional gifts for friends
write on back of this order form.

To: Name _____
       YOUR FRIEND'S NAME

Address _____

CITY   STATE   ZIP

My Salutation: _____

_____

ORDERING INFORMATION
Please check the boxes of your choice (if more than one, please insert quantity)

Also available from Creativity Unlimited:

★ **BOOKS**
- ☐ INSIDES OUT ....$ 6.95
- ☐ GREAT RELATIONS 9.95
- ☐ HYPNOSIS (Smile On Your Face & $ In Your Pocket) 9.95
- ☐ SEX & OTHER TOUCHY SUBJECTS 14.95

★ **SELF HYPNOSIS CASSETTES**
- ☐ NO MORE SUGAR JUNKIE $10
- ☐ YES, I CAN QUIT SMOKING $10
- ☐ FLIGHT ATTENDANT WELL-BEING $10
- ☐ SLEEP, BEAUTIFUL SLEEP $10
- ☐ PEACE AND CALM $10
- ☐ YES! I CAN $10
- ☐ LOSE WEIGHT $10
- ☐ THE MONEY TAPE $10

★ **KIDS**
- ☐ MOMMY BUNNY'S GOING TO WORK $10
- ☐ U R WHAT U EAT $10

★ **MUSIC AND SONG**
- ☐ DEEP INTO A CALMING OCEAN $10
- ☐ SEX & OTHER TOUCHY SUBJECTS $10

SUBTOTAL

(California residents add 7¢ per dollar sales tax)
Foreign Countries please add $1.00 to the price fo each publication.

PLUS $2.50 POSTAGE AND HANDLING PER ITEM

TOTAL

ALLOW 4-6 WEEKS FOR DELIVERY

FOR FAST ORDERING: CALL (213) 541-4844
Payment Method

- ☐ Check/Money Order
- ☐ Charge   ☐ VISA   ☐ MasterCard

Card No. _____

Expiration Date _____

Card Holders Signature

Please complete this page and mail to:

CREATIVITY UNLIMITED PRESS
30819 Casilina, Rancho Palos Verdes, CA 90274

PLEASE PRINT

NAME _____

ADDRESS _____

CITY _____ STATE _____

ZIP _____ PHONE ( ) _____

CREATIVITY UNLIMITED